# The Kaufmann Diet Guide

## Eating The Right Foods to Feel Great

Doug Kaufmann

Readandlearn LLC
Rockwall, TX

Published by:
Readandlearn LLC
Rockwall, TX 75087
www.knowthecause.com

ISBN: 978-0-9827984-3-0

First Printing

All material herein is for informational purposes only and does not take the place of professional advice from your healthcare provider. Approaches described are not offered as cures, prescriptions, or diagnoses. Information is a compiled report of existing data and/or research. The authors and publisher assume no responsibility in the use of this information. Consult your doctor before using any presented information as a form of treatment.

Manufactured in the United States
Cover Design by Evan Kaufmann

Special thanks to Joy Miller, Abby Miller, Lindsey Crouch, and Melissa Henig, all of whom spent much time in cooking and assembling the recipes. In addition to recipe contributions, Damon Black and Kristin Hoedebeck worked tirelessly on concept and design.
Thank you all!

# Introduction to The Kaufmann Diet Guide

www.theantifungaldiet.com
www.knowthecause.com

Little did I know in the 1970s what my diet discovery would reveal. I was a combat action-trained hospital corpsman and served in that capacity with the 7th Marines in Vietnam. I returned home with the most bizarre symptoms one could ever imagine and attributed those symptoms to parasites I might have gotten into while in Vietnam. A few years later, I learned that there are many different kinds of parasites that can infect we humans, one of which was fungi. I thought parasites were worms, yet to my amazement, I discovered that the jungle rot on my arms and legs had somehow passed through my skin and was now causing my misery. To hasten this misery, I was 21 years old when returning from Vietnam, and that is the legal drinking age where I lived. I now know with certainty that my pasta, bread, cereals, sugar, donuts, and alcohol actually had fueled what jungle rot may have initiated.

During the past 47 years, I have studied single-celled fungi (yeast) and other fungi more than most people, and one thing that will help readers of this book is this one fact: Fungi parasitize humans and then thrive inside them when their diets are high in fungi's favorite food—carbohydrates. You may have purchased this book because someone told you how great they feel on The Kaufmann Diet. You want to feel that way, too! Thank you!

About 2500 years ago, Hippocrates, the father of western medicine, argued that food could actually be medicinal, if it was the right food. Welcome to The Kaufmann Diet, the anti-fungal diet. This diet eliminates the many commonly eaten foods in our diets that are either impregnated with fungus or actually feed fungal conditions we might already have. My challenge decades ago was to develop a healthy and nutritious diet around these food exclusions. Thousands of people are now benefitting from The Kaufmann Diet. Check with your doctor as he/she knows your medical history, then commit to this diet for 30 days. No, it won't cure your medical condition, but if you're feeling so much better, more of the same might have you feeling dramatically better. Most importantly, within a month, you will finally know why you have been suffering for so long. Fungal diseases are called the great masqueraders, in that they can mimic virtually every disease known to doctors, including cancer and diabetes. Relax, read, and learn!

# Table of Contents

# CHAPTER 1

# Getting Started on The Kaufmann Diet

The Kaufmann Diet is designed to do two things. First, it is designed to starve disease-causing yeast and fungus living inside your body that may be contributing to your symptoms or diseases. Yes, fungus can do that! To accomplish this, The Kaufmann Diets restrict sugar and many carbohydrates that we commonly eat. As parasites, once inside our bodies, fungi thrive on pasta, bread, sugar, corn, and even alcohol. Since fungi tend to dominate our human cells, they slowly alter your eating choices to satisfy their own existence. Before you know it, you are hiding sugar everywhere, and even the smell of freshly baked bread is enough to cause salivation. Mind you, this isn't you craving these foods; it's fungi demanding them. The Kaufmann Diet eliminates foods like these and also foods that are impregnated with these fungi and their poisons, known as mycotoxins. Fungal contamination in seemingly good food is actually quite a common problem in American diets, according to those who study fungi and our food system. Second and of equal importance, The Kaufmann Diet is designed to offer you excellent, nutritionally dense foods while fungal starving is being accomplished.

The Kaufmann Diet achieves these two things largely by eliminating many of the foods that are common in people's every day diets. The Kaufmann Diet eliminates the aforementioned foods, in addition to anything with added sugar, potatoes, legumes, many of the sweeter varieties of fruits, and foods that are at risk for mycotoxin contamination, such as peanuts, mushrooms, or anything made with yeast.

After studying The Kaufmann Diets initially, many people wonder what is left to eat. Herein lies the utility of this cookbook; this cookbook focuses on Kaufmann 1 & 2 approved foods in lieu of the foods that are restricted on the diet. The Kaufmann Diet encourages lean organic meats, eggs, certain dairy products, lots of vegetables, certain fruits, nuts, seeds, and healthy fats and oils. (*Foods that are excluded and permitted are discussed in greater detail in The Kaufmann Diets section of the book.*)

On the surface, The Kaufmann Diet is similar to other popular diets, such as Adkins, ketogenic, or paleo diets. There is one key difference, however; while many of the foods permitted and excluded on these diets are similar to the foods permitted and excluded on The Kaufmann Diet, none of these diets address the role of yeast and fungi in health problems. Foods that are commonly contaminated with fungal poisons (mycotoxins) or that would feed an underlying fungal infection are still permitted on these other types of diets. Therefore, while these diets might assist in bolstering health, they ultimately never address what may potentially be the root cause of many health problems: fungi and their poisons.

While The Kaufmann Diet is perfectly healthy on its own, it is easy to tailor The Kaufmann Diet to other diets, if you so choose. In other words, you can still do paleo, ketogenic, Adkins, or even a vegan diet and still stay within the guidelines of The Kaufmann Diet framework. Ultimately, the issue is avoiding foods that are contaminated with fungal poisons or that would exacerbate a yeast or fungal infection.

It is important to note that The Kaufmann Diets are more about what you eat rather than how much you eat. The Kaufmann Diet does not necessarily encourage calorie counting or portion control; on The Kaufmann Diet, as long as you are eating foods that are within the dietary guidelines, within reason, you can have as much as you want. There is never a reason to be hungry while on The Kaufmann Diet. Certain fungi, like penicillin, are known to cause weight gain. Eating the allowable eggs and turkey bacon for breakfast on The Kaufmann Diet does not promote weight gain, because these foods do not feed fungus. Often, after a period of time on the diet, many people feel extremely satisfied with what they are eating *and* lose significant weight despite paying little attention to portion control or number of calories.

## Growing into the Kaufmann Lifestyle

Many people begin following The Kaufmann Diet to determine if their symptoms are linked to fungus. Once a fungal link to health problems is determined, most choose to make The Kaufmann Diet a long-term lifestyle, not just an experimental diet that is adhered to for a short period of time. Many dieters feel so good after a period of time on the diet that it simply makes sense to continue the diet as a way of life. To that end, there are some strategies that you can regularly employ to help turn The Kaufmann Diet into The Kaufmann Lifestyle.

## Meal and Food Preparation

Obviously, many people will be spending more time in the kitchen than they are accustom to, which can be intimidating, initially. Herein, again, lies the utility of this cookbook. You can, however, limit the time you must spend in the kitchen by preparing food in advance. It is a good idea to cook in bulk, refrigerate or freeze leftovers, and use these to create multiple meals from a single cooking session. Slicing up fruits and vegetables and keeping them visible in the refrigerator makes for healthy, attractive, and quick snacks when you are feeling peckish. This also eliminates the need to spend extra time in the kitchen.

Often people fall victim to buying too much fresh produce or fresh meat only to see that food spoil and be tossed out. To avoid wasting food and money, try breaking up your trips to the grocery store. Instead of one big trip per week, try to make multiple small trips per week, only buying what you know you will eat. This will ensure you have a steady supply of fresh, nutrient-dense food available and ultimately make eating at home even more affordable. This may seem inconvenient for some, but given the pivotal role that the food you eat can play in your health, this can be an important habit to cultivate, both for your health and your finances.

## Reading and Understanding Food Labels and Marketing

Becoming an informed consumer is an important part of The Kaufmann Diet and cultivating The Kaufmann Lifestyle. Shopping for produce is a good example of why this is important. Often, foods such as produce can be labeled as "natural" or "all-natural", which does not really have any meaning. In other words, there is no set of standards that a product must meet in order to be labeled as natural.

On the other hand, organic produce must meet specific standards, including being cultivated without an array of harmful pesticides, in order to be labeled as such. (Look for the USDA Organic label, which is the gold standard for organic produce.) True organic food is, by its very definition, non-GMO (genetically modified organisms) food. Opt for organic produce when possible, but in the event that it is not, do not let that deter you from enjoying vegetables and fruits that are permitted on The Kaufmann Diet. Non-organic kale is preferable to organic potatoes on this diet, for example.

Farmers markets and CSAs (community supported agriculture) are also good options when it comes to getting the freshest produce. Many people now opt to cultivate their own gardens, which can be a good option for some.

**Reading Labels**

Marketing is a powerful tool; with the public's interest in health and nutrition at an all-time high, food purveyors often do whatever they can to market their food products as health-promoting. However, many of the products that are marketed as "healthy" are highly processed foods that contain ingredients not permitted on The Kaufmann Diet.

Ideally, most of the food that you buy should not contain an ingredients list at all; a bunch of broccoli or carrots, for example, is not grown with an ingredients list! Most of what you buy at the grocery store should be whole foods, unaltered from their natural state or minimally processed, at the most.

Some foods, however, will come with labels, and it is important to understand what you are reading when you read these labels. Circumstances will often dictate that you do buy some types of prepackaged foods. This is perfectly fine, but it is important to become adept at reading labels and discerning which of these foods are best for your diet.

The first ingredient listed always comprises the bulk of what is packaged. Conversely, the final ingredient listed is present in the smallest amount within the ingredients that make up the final product. It is important that each ingredient listed is a real food that complies with The Kaufmann Diet. Here is a list (albeit, not comprehensive) of ingredients to avoid as best you can:

- Corn syrup
- High fructose corn syrup
- Fructose
- Agave
- Evaporated cane juice
- Sugar
- Anything ending in "-ose" (sucrose, dextrose, fructose, etc.)
- Sodium nitrate or nitrite
- Yeast
- Torula yeast
- Hydrolyzed yeast
- Hydrogenated oil
- Gluten
- MSG (monosodium glutamate)
- Anything containing corn, wheat, soy, peanuts or anything derived from those ingredients

It is also important to remember that products like pre-made baking mixes—even if they are gluten free—might still contain ingredients such as corn or soy that are not permitted on The Kaufmann Diet. Foods such as lunch meats, beef jerky, and other processed meat products also often contain ingredients like sugar, wheat, or corn that should be avoided. Buying meats without those ingredients is possible.

Ultimately, it is simply important to cultivate mindfulness about what is in the food you are eating. Read labels, and know where your food comes from as best you can.

## Fresh Food List

Fresh, whole foods should comprise the majority of your food intake on The Kaufmann Diets. These simply are where you will find an abundance of nutrition, anti-fungal nutrients, and the nutrients necessary to maintain excellent health. For many, this can be a departure from how you are accustom to eating; gone are the processed and boxed foods, fast foods, frozen meals, and all of the junk foods that many people sadly rely on for nutrition. Instead, you are incorporating a wide variety of vegetables, some healthy fruits, unprocessed meats, nuts, seeds, and healthy oils.

For many, it takes some time to get accustomed to buying fresh food, because it goes bad! Fresh food is not laden with preservatives, so it does have a shelf life. The best advice is to not buy too much of anything when you are first starting out; this prevents waste of food and money. With time, it becomes easier to learn what to buy and how much to buy of each food item.

This fresh food list can act as a baseline grocery store list for those eating on The Kaufmann Diet.

**Fruit:**

Avocados
Berries (fresh or frozen)
Grapefruit
Green Apples
Limes
Lemons
Tomatoes

**Vegetables:**

Bell Peppers
Broccoli
Carrots
Cauliflower
Celery

Cucumbers
Fresh herbs
Garlic
Leafy greens
Onions
Parsnips
Seasonal squash
Sweet potatoes (Kaufmann 2)
Zucchini

**Meat:**
Beef
Chicken
Pork
Seafood
Turkey

**Refrigerated:**
Almond milk (unsweetened)
Butter
Cashew milk (unsweetened)
Cream cheese
Eggs
Heavy whipping cream
Plain, unsweetened yogurt with active cultures
Real sour cream

# Pantry List

Often, in the pantry you will find a wide variety of foods, such as crackers, chips, snack foods, processed fare, and grain products that should ideally be eliminated from your diet. These simply constitute a temptation to slip back into old ways of eating. While The Kaufmann Diet can be extremely effective at promoting excellent health, its efficacy is diminished the more these kinds of foods are kept in the diet.

When you are on The Kaufmann Diet, it is imperative that you keep your pantry stocked with foods that are permitted on your diet. To assist with this, we have compiled a list of foods that are good to keep on hand in the pantry. These foods do not require refrigeration and have a reasonable shelf life; they can be considered staples of your diet and fixtures in your pantry.

Trading in whatever unhealthy fare you might have in your pantry for foods like these will ensure not only that you will never go hungry, but you will not be tempted to fall off the diet.

**Sweeteners:**
Manuka Honey (Kaufmann 2)
Maple Syrup (Kaufmann 2)
Stevia – granulated and liquid
Xylitol

**Nut Milks:**
Almond
Cashew
Coconut

**Spices:**
Cinnamon
Garlic
Ginger
Onion
Pepper
Sea Salt
Vanilla Extract

**Canned/Jar Items:**

Apple cider vinegar
Black olives
Canned whole tomatoes
Chickpeas (Kaufmann 2)
Chicken and beef broth
Nut butters (almond, cashew)
Tomato paste
Wild-caught canned tuna and salmon

**Oils:**

Avocado oil
Coconut oil
Grape seed oil
Macadamia nut oil
Olive oil
Sesame oil

**Flours:**

Almond
Arrowroot
Coconut
Tapioca

**Pseudo Grains/Grains:**

Quinoa
Quinoa flakes
Lentils (*Kaufmann 2*)
Oats (*Kaufmann 2*)

**Raw Nuts/Seeds:**

Almonds
Brazil nuts
Cashews
Filberts
Macadamia nuts
Pecans
Walnuts

Chia Seeds
Flax Seeds
Pumpkin Seeds

## Anti-Fungal Foods

The Kaufmann Diets include a wide array of natural, whole foods. These include varieties of vegetables, meats, poultry, fish, eggs, nuts, seeds, some fruit, and limited dairy. All of the foods on The Kaufmann Diet are allowed for two reasons. First, any food included on the diet should be free of mycotoxin contamination and should not be known to feed any disease-causing yeasts or fungi (yeasts are single celled fungi). When you are following The Kaufmann Diet, you are literally preventing yeasts and fungi that might be living inside your body from getting their favorite foods; primarily, this means eliminating sugar and simple carbohydrates. This goal can be achieved simply by relegating what you eat to the foods allowed on the diets. Second, any foods included in The Kaufmann Diets should be very healthy and contain a high nutritional content.

You have likely heard that plants contain nutrients called phenolic compounds. We know these are beneficial, but likely many of us do not necessarily know why. In 2015, *The International Journal of Current Science Research* (Volume 1, Issue 6, Nov. 2015) stated, "All plants possess phenolic compounds but the amount may vary." Two years earlier (April, 2013), the *Canadian Journal of Plant Pathology* stated that "…it has been demonstrated that phenolic compounds have anti-fungal properties." When you eat plants, you are getting tiny (plant doses) amounts of plant anti-fungals; remember this the next time you eat fruits and vegetables.

Think about it this way. If a seed survives the germination process and goes on to grow and flourish, it is because it was protected from harmful germs within the soil. Because you eat it, now you are protected, too! Fungi are, after all, ubiquitous, and plants must exhibit some defense against fungi in order to survive and grow. Similarly, nutrients like omega 3 fatty acids found in fish, eggs, and grass-fed beef exhibit anti-fungal activity, as well. Ultimately, while there are many foods that posses anti-fungal qualities, there are some that excel at this.

### Garlic

Garlic possesses a wide variety of health benefits, but among them are its anti-fungal properties. Garlic contains allicin among other components that make it potently anti-fungal. Raw garlic is excellent towards this end.

## Salmon and Other Fish

Wild caught salmon and other cold water fish are rich in omega 3 fatty acids. We all know that omega 3 fatty acids are beneficial for heart health, brain health, and skin health, among other tissues. I am suggesting that the very reason these fatty acids are so healthy for our tissues is because they possess these wonderful anti-fungal properties.

## Coconut

Coconut is among the most potently anti-fungal foods, from the flesh, to the milk, to the fatty oil. Coconut oil may be extra potently anti-fungal. Coconut is rich in lauric and caprylic acid, both of which are known to fight fungus; while it is obviously an excellent choice for cooking, it is also beneficial topically.

## Carrots

Carrots are rich in a wide variety of phytonutrients and carotenoids, but particularly, carrots contain a powerful fungus-fighting nutrient called falcarinol. Fresh carrot juice is a good option once in a while on The Kaufmann Diet for the inherent nutritional value and anti-fungal properties.

## Nuts and Seeds

Nuts and seeds that are rich in omega 3s, such as walnuts, pumpkin seeds, or flax seeds, can be beneficial against fungi and yeasts. Know that foods within shells can be contaminated with fungi. When buying, try to find nuts and seeds with their shells intact.

## Onions

Onions contain sulfuric compounds that exhibit anti-fungal properties.

## Olive Oil

Of all the oils, scientists tell us that olive oil is among the healthiest you can consume. It possess anti-fungal properties that are beneficial both topically and as part of your diet. Be careful when cooking with olive oil, however, as the smoke point is typically lower than other oils. Cold-pressed, extra virgin olive oil is best.

# Herbs & Spices

Herbs and spices have been used for millennia as medicinal remedies, but it is only in recent years that science has affirmed their use for certain health problems. For some maladies, we are learning that herbs and spices confer as much benefit as certain medications, both over the counter and prescription. This certainly validates what Hippocrates, the father of medicine, said about 2,500 years ago: "Let food be your medicine and medicine be your food."

Certainly, herbs and spices constitute an important part of cooking, too; herbs and spices are largely how we impart delicious flavor to our food. This is important; the healthiest diet in the world is useless if it is impossible to follow. Seasoning food with herbs and spices is one way to make your food taste delicious and satisfying. We should be using more herbs and spices in our foods, both for the health benefits and the flavor.

It shouldn't surprise you to learn that herbs and spices also happen to be among the most potent anti-fungals we have available to us. While many are available in supplement form (and these are an important part of an anti-fungal program) why not enjoy them as part of our diet, as well? We only stand to benefit from their liberal use.

These are among the most potent anti-fungal herbs and spices:

## Cinnamon

Many people think of cinnamon as a flavoring for sweet treats, but its utility extends far beyond that. Cinnamon is a potent anti-fungal; in some studies, cinnamon performed better at killing yeast than certain prescription anti-fungal medicines, such as Diflucan. (1) This makes cinnamon a powerful tool for The Kaufmann Diet. Of the two types of cinnamon, ceylon cinnamon seems to be the best variety to use, in terms of the health benefits. In addition to being potently anti-fungal, cinnamon is thought to reduce inflammation, promote heart health, and help regulate blood sugar.

## Clove

Cloves have also been studied for their ability to work against fungi, including strains of fungus resistant to prescription drugs. Outside of being delicious, cloves exhibit potent, natural anti-inflammatory activity. Cloves are naturally anti-septic and act as a numbing agent, making them beneficial for some types of pain. It is thought that cloves protect against certain cancers as well, particularly oral cancers.

## Ginger

Certain compounds in ginger, such as gingerols and shogaols, are thought to be anti-fungal. Ginger is also great for those who suffer from stomach problems and is an excellent remedy for an upset stomach. Ginger also protects heart health and may provide anti-cancer benefits.

## Oregano

Oregano and oregano oil have been used for centuries as medicinal remedies. Oregano's anti-fungal properties make it an important addition to your spice rack; it is among the more potent, natural anti-fungals available to us. In addition to being an excellent yeast-killer, oregano is beneficial for upper-respiratory problems, acts as an anti-inflammatory, and has anti-bacterial properties.

## Turmeric

Turmeric has been studied extensively in recent years; turmeric and its active component known as curcumin have subsequently become well known for their disease fighting ability. From its anti-inflammatory uses, to its anti-cancer properties, turmeric is something we should all think about using regularly. Turmeric and curcumin are also potent anti-fungals.

---

*References:*

(1) Goel, Nidhi. "Antifungal Activity of Cinnamon Oil and Olive Oil against Candida Spp. Isolated from Blood Stream Infections." *Journal Of Clinical And Diagnostic Research*, 2016, doi:10.7860/jcdr/2016/19958.8339.

## 5 Tips on Sticking to the Diet

For some people, sticking to The Kaufmann Diet is difficult, particularly at first. For most Americans, The Kaufmann Diet represents a completely different way of eating than they are accustom to; many of the foods people eat every day are eliminated. Changing your dietary habits is difficult, but it is possible. And, once you begin to see and feel the effects of eating a healthy, nutritious diet, you likely will never want to go back to previous ways of eating.

Here are a few tips for sticking to the diet as you begin.

### Purge Your Fridge…

… and your pantry… and your office… and anywhere else you keep food or snacks that might not be on your diet. Keeping unhealthy food out of reach is a good way to ensure you do not give in to cravings when they hit. Instead, fill your refrigerator and pantry with foods that are on your diet. In places that you keep snacks, replace unhealthy foods with healthy snacks like almonds, cashews, green apples, and carrots. Individual cups of plain, unsweetened yogurt with active cultures are a quick, easy, and filling way to fight off cravings.

### Skip Eating Out When Possible

Eating out is convenient, but one pays a price, both financially and with your health. Unfortunately, it is very tough to eat healthy when you eat at a restaurant; you can never be certain about what is in the food you are eating. Try instead—at least, initially—to only eat at home, and skip the restaurants.

### Plan Ahead

Cooking in advance for the week is an easy way to always have healthy food ready to heat up. Making menus and sticking to them is an easy way to make sure all the food you eat fits within the dietary framework. Planning ahead simply allows you to make sure you will be sticking to your diet with each meal, and it allows you to plan on eating foods you both enjoy and that fit within your dietary framework. It also gives you less of an excuse to hit the closest drive-thru.

## Become a Food Carrier

Maybe you haven't done this since 4th grade! Many of us fall victim to eating whatever is around out of convenience; do not let circumstances derail you from your health goals. Make a habit of carrying healthy food with you if you know you are going to be away from home. This can mean bringing your lunch to work or packing healthy snacks for a trip. Invest in quality food-carrying equipment, such as a high-quality cooler or water bottle. With all the products designed for these purposes, carrying your own food has never been easier.

## Find a Few Meals You Enjoy on the Diet, and Rotate Them.

To this end, this cookbook becomes extremely valuable. It has never been easier to find Kaufmann Diet-friendly recipes. In the pages of this book, you will find meals that you and your family can enjoy; enjoy them regularly! When you eat foods you enjoy, slipping into old eating habits becomes far less attractive.

# CHAPTER 2

# The Kaufmann Lifestyle in the Kitchen

The Kaufmann Diets are designed to starve pathogenic yeasts and fungi and mitigate the risk of exposure to fungal poisons, called mycotoxins. To this end, the diets can be very effective. However, it is important to include the diets into a lifestyle that supports health and actively avoids fungal exposure. This is what is known as the Kaufmann Lifestyle.

The Kaufmann Lifestyle—which includes The Kaufmann Diets—is a comprehensive approach to healthy living. It includes diet, exercise, supplementation, mitigating stress, and getting healthy amounts of sleep. It is has implications for where you live and how clean your indoor space is; it requires being cognizant of the possibility of mold contamination in your home or place of work.

The idea is that when multiple facets of your lifestyle work in harmony, you put yourself in a position to best live an anti-fungal life. Good health, I believe, will ensue. I have long defined "health" as being actively anti-fungal!

Good health often begins in the kitchen. While The Kaufmann Diet dictates what foods to avoid and what foods to enjoy, the Kaufmann Lifestyle has implications for the quality of those foods, how they are prepared, and how to regularly enjoy them.

## Explanation of Ingredients

For many people, The Kaufmann Diets are their first introduction to eating in a way that supports good health rather than detracting from it. The Kaufmann Diets encourage a wide variety of whole, unprocessed, healthy foods. This cookbook provides a wonderful array of ways to prepare those healthy foods.

While The Kaufmann Diet mostly emphasizes the types of foods that are included (and excluded), the quality of those foods that are included on the diet is important, also.

For brevity's sake, recipes contained in this book do not go to great lengths to describe the quality of the ingredients in each recipe, but it should be understood that shopping for the highest quality ingredients is always recommended. For example, if a recipe calls for olive oil, you can assume that using extra-virgin, cold-pressed olive oil, preferably organic, is encouraged.

While the quality of ingredients is not stressed in each recipe, it is good to understand what is implied.

### Produce

It is best to shop for organic produce when possible. Look for the USDA Organic seal on any organic foods, as this is the gold standard for organic produce in the United States. Organic produce is far less likely to be contaminated with dangerous pesticides. If organic is unavailable, or unaffordable, it's perfectly acceptable to buy conventional. Regardless, always wash produce thoroughly before preparing.

Remember that natural is not the same as organic; the labeling of foods as "natural" really does not amount to anything other than clever marketing.

### Salt, Pepper, Herbs and Spices

Pink Himalayan salt or sea salt is encouraged, though these might not be specifically mentioned in recipes. Table salt is fine to use too, but the mineral content is not as high. Table salt, however, is fortified with iodine, an important nutrient for thyroid health. Cracking pepper as you use it is preferred, though recipes will not say specifically to use freshly ground pepper. Fresh herbs and spices are encouraged, and organic is preferred when possible.

### Oils

For any oil, look for extra-virgin, cold-pressed, and organic varieties. Avoid any refined oils, particularly hydrogenated oils and vegetable oils.

## Meats

Look for grass-fed, grass-finished, organic varieties of beef, bison, pork, and lamb. These are fed a natural diet consisting of grass, which is what their bodies are designed to consume. The result is far healthier and nutritious meat. These products are rich in omega 3 fats and a variety of nutrients not found abundantly in conventionally raised meat. I encourage everyone to support local farms that enable their cattle to eat (and be finished on) grass. Government allowances for beef call for 75% of cattle to be started on grass, then "finished" with a diet that is high in corn and other grains. This is done to encourage fattening of the cattle.

I also have to question the U.S. government's allowance of an estrogen-mimicking growth hormone called Zeranol, or Ralgro into our meat (beef and lamb) supply. The European Union does not allow this hormone in their meat supply, nor will they buy any North American meat that was grown with the use of Ralgro. Since this hormone is a growth promoter, it is my understanding that American farmers are using this hormone in lieu of antibiotics to fatten their cattle.

## Poultry

Free-range, organic poultry, such as chicken and turkey, is encouraged in lieu of conventionally raised varieties. The same goes for eggs.

## Fish and Seafood

Wild caught fish and seafood are overwhelmingly preferred to farmed fish. Farmed fish are notoriously contaminated with toxins and are often fed a diet rich in grain and corn. Look for responsibly sourced varieties when possible.

## Reading Labels

It is important to read labels on any foods you buy at the grocery store. Even seemingly healthy foods, such as almond butter, often have added sugar or other ingredients. Many foods might have added wheat or corn components. These foods should be avoided, even if they are marketed as healthy.

## Organic Produce

Eating fresh produce is one of the very best ways to get nutrients to support optimal health. However, when it comes to buying produce, buying 100% organic can be very expensive. The good news is that you do not necessarily need to buy organic produce, exclusively. There are, however, certain fruits and vegetables that you should always consider buying organic.

A good rule of thumb when buying organic is to think of the fruits and vegetables that have thin skins. These have less protection from harmful pesticides and chemicals that can more easily penetrate through thin skin and absorb into the fruit or vegetable.

Pesticides can have real health risks, especially for children and those with health concerns. According to studies, this list of produce has the highest pesticide load when grown conventionally, making them the most important to buy organic varieties of, or to grow them organically, yourself.

These are some foods that you should always try to buy organic and are Kaufmann 1 Diet-approved:

- Green Apples
- Blueberries
- Strawberries
- Tomatoes
- Cucumbers
- Celery
- Spinach
- Kale
- Collard Greens
- Lettuce
- Sweet Bell Peppers
- Hot Peppers

The decision is always yours, but having this information is beneficial for protecting you and your family from harmful pesticides and herbicides.

## The Benefits of Raw Foods

Eating raw foods can make your skin glow, give you more energy, promote clearer thinking, and help you lose weight naturally. Raw foods are whole foods that come in their original, natural state; these include foods that are unheated, unprocessed, and unaltered in anyway. Our bodies are designed to recognize and assimilate these types of foods that are found in nature.

Raw foods include raw fruits and vegetables, soaked and sprouted nuts, seeds, fresh herbs, and tonic herbs. Eating raw food allows our bodies to absorb essential enzymes, probiotics, vitamins, and minerals in their most natural form. These building blocks provide our bodies with better hydration, lessen inflammation, and improve digestion.

Enzymes, in particular, are vital to our health. They make life possible; every process, from blinking our eyes, to smiling, to thinking is made possible by enzymes. Enzymes are the catalysts for all biochemical processes in the body. Enzymes assist in digesting food easily and are systemic healers. Enzymes, however, are easily destroyed by heat; eating raw foods is the best way to ensure you maintain an adequate supply of these powerful catalysts.

Raw foods are often packed with numerous beneficial microorganisms. When food is grown in an organic, sustainable manner, the resulting microorganisms are pro-life. In other words, they are probiotics; probiotics are the beneficial organisms that support a strong immune system.

Raw foods often have a higher water content than processed foods, which assists in keeping the body cool and hydrated. Hydration keeps you glowing, youthful, and vibrant. It is important to eat your water as well as drink it!

Raw foods are simply something you should enjoy in abundance, and they should constitute a substantial part of your Kaufmann Diet.

**Certain foods, such as pork, and other meats, poultry, shellfish and others should never be consumed raw, particularly if you suffer from any sort of health problems. Consult your physician if you have questions about consuming any sort of raw food.*

## Super Foods

The term superfood implies a food that is especially rich in nutrients; this idea has been around for a while, but there is not necessarily a consensus on what constitutes a superfood, nor is there a universally agreed upon list of what those foods are. Certainly, there is a good deal of overlap on many lists of so-called superfoods, because some foods simply stand out among others in terms of their nutrition.

Within the parameters of The Kaufmann Diet, certain foods stand out from others in terms of their nutritional value, as well. While the overwhelming majority of the foods permitted on The Kaufmann Diet are whole foods with lots of inherent nutritional value, we can confidently say that some foods contain a greater nutritional value than others. These are foods we should likely be incorporating into our diet regularly in order to benefit from the abundance of nutrition therein.

### Broccoli

Broccoli is rich in a variety of nutrients, like vitamin K, vitamin C, chromium, and folate. Broccoli is also a good source of fiber—a nutrient many people fail to get enough of in their diet. Other phytonutrients found in broccoli, such as sulforaphane, are known to promote health; these compounds are anti-inflammatory and may help to prevent cancer. Sulforaphane, itself, is known to kill a bacteria that causes stomach ulcers that can ultimately lead to stomach cancer. *(Brussels sprouts and cabbage also contain good amounts of sulforaphane.)*

### Avocados

Avocados are an important source of healthy fats and fiber, but they are also rich in a variety of other nutrients, including pantothenic acid, vitamin K, copper, folate, vitamin B6, and vitamin E. Avocados are known to provide cardiovascular support and might be beneficial for insulin control. Many nutrients in avocados are known to fight inflammation and help repair oxidative damage, as well.

### Carrots

Though beta carotene often gets mentioned the most, there are over 400 carotenoids in carrots. Carrots are also rich in lutein, an antioxidant known to support eye health. Falcarinol, however, is the potent anti-fungal nutrient that stands out; the anti-fungal properties of carrots are what make carrot juice an encouraged beverage on The Kaufmann Diet.

## Garlic

Garlic is rich in antioxidants and is known to support heart health. Garlic acts as a vasodilator, opening blood vessels and allowing blood to flow more freely. Garlic contains a variety of potently anti-fungal compounds, making it particularly useful on The Kaufmann Diet.

## Blueberries

Blueberries are a well known source of antioxidants, and they are also rich in vitamin K, vitamin C, manganese, and fiber. Many of the nutrients in blueberries are known to be anti-inflammatory and are thought to prevent cancer.

## Spinach

Spinach is high in a wide variety of nutrients, including vitamins A, C, E, and K; B vitamins; manganese; folate; magnesium; iron; copper; calcium; and potassium. Eating spinach is a lot like swallowing a multivitamin. It is also a green, therefore rich in chlorophyl—a powerful, detoxifying substance.

## Walnuts

Walnuts are high in fiber and healthy fats, including omega 3 fatty acids. Walnuts are also rich in a variety of other phytonutrients, including tannins, polyphenols, and flavonoids. Walnuts have been shown to have anti-inflammatory properties and are a good source of vitamin E.

## Almonds

Almonds are rich in biotin, vitamin E, copper, manganese, phosphorous, and magnesium. These are a good source of protein and healthy fats. Almonds might provide benefits for the cardiovascular system and protection against diabetes, as well.

## Coconuts

Coconut is perhaps the only food that humans can survive on exclusively; coconut water provides hydration while the flesh provides nutrition. Coconut is rich in healthy fats and a variety of anti-fungal nutrients, making it a valuable addition The Kaufmann Diet.

## Apple Cider Vinegar

Vinegar is a staple ingredient in most kitchens, but on The Kaufmann Diet, vinegar is mostly eliminated. Why is this?

Vinegar is created via the fermentation of alcohol (ethanol) by acetic acid bacteria. Vinegar consists of anywhere between 5-20% acetic acid, water, and other flavoring agents. Vinegar can be created with virtually any liquid containing alcohol.

White vinegar is widely used in baking and cooking. It is distilled from a high ABV (alcohol by volume) spirit that is derived from grain. As such, it runs the risk of mycotoxin contamination. In fact, since vinegars are distilled from alcoholic liquids, all have the risk of mycotoxin contamination. Most yeast-fermented products, including most vinegars, kefir, kombucha, and any sort of alcohol beverage, are discouraged on The Kaufmann Diets.

### Apple Cider Vinegar (ACV) on The Kaufmann Diet

The one exception to this rule is apple cider vinegar. Apple cider vinegar is largely touted for its health benefits; proponents of apple cider vinegar claim that it can help you lose weight, prevent cancer, help control blood sugar, and help lower cholesterol. Apple cider vinegar also might be beneficial for the skin and hair, and it can also be beneficial against harmful bacteria.

There is another component of apple cider vinegar that makes it acceptable—and even beneficial—on The Kaufmann Diet. Malic acid is a component found in apple cider vinegar, and there is evidence that it is potently anti-fungal. Published studies have found malic acid to be a useful fungicide against several species of fungus and yeast, including Candida.

Because of the inherent health benefits and the anti-fungal properties of apple cider vinegar, it is encouraged on The Kaufmann Diet to the exclusion of all other vinegars. It is fairly easy to incorporate into cooking; simply substitute apple cider vinegar for other vinegars in recipes.

Some people do choose to use apple cider vinegar supplementally, and this is encouraged while on The Kaufmann Diet, as it is a potent anti-fungal. Usually, a teaspoon in water daily is enough to glean the anti-fungal benefits of ACV, and it can safely be rotated into your regimen with other natural anti-fungal supplements.

Look for organic, unfiltered varieties. The cloudier varieties contain the "mother", which is comprised of proteins, enzymes, and beneficial bacteria; these are the best varieties to search for when they are available. The mother is thought to contain many of the health-promoting properties of apple cider vinegar.

## Converting Your Favorite Foods to The Kaufmann Diets

New to The Kaufmann Diet? No worries, here are some helpful quick tips that will help you transition in the kitchen.

### Flours

Eliminating grains is one of the main focuses of The Kaufmann Diet. For many, that poses a challenge to convert your family's favorite meals, snacks, deserts, etc. all while staying within the guidelines of The Kaufmann Diet. There are plenty of flour substitutions that do not include wheat, corn, or rye. Nearly every grocery store carries multiple types of flours that are Kaufmann Diet–friendly, and a few are listed here:

#### Almond Flour

Almond flour is good for baking things that need flavor and density like cookies, pie crusts, and muffins.

#### Coconut Flour

Coconut flour is good for moist cakes and muffins.

#### Tapioca Flour and Arrowroot Flour

These are beneficial for thickening sauces and gravies.

#### Buckwheat Flour

Buckwheat flour is good for pancakes or breads, just use double leavening agents like baking soda and baking powder.

**Quinoa and Seed Flours**
These are good for crispy, textured coatings.

**Brown Rice Flour**
Brown rice flour is permitted on The Kaufmann 2 Diet and is good for breading and frying.

If you are looking for pre-packaged, gluten-free baking mixes, check the label to look for hidden, unapproved ingredients.

## Sweeteners

The world of sweeteners seems to be expanding daily, but most are not Kaufmann Diet-friendly. This is because fungus loves most sweeteners. Make sure to read the labels for hidden ingredients and ingredients ending with "-ose", such as sucrose, fructose, etc. Find which Kaufmann Diet–friendly sweetener works best with your palate.

**Stevia**
This is the most-used sweetener on The Kaufmann Diet. This product comes from the leaves of the stevia plant and is 30-150 times as sweet as sugar, so be careful to add it to dishes according to your taste preference. Too much may actually make the end product taste bitter instead of sweet. Stevia is heat-stable, does not ferment, and is pH-stable. Liquid stevia seems to work best when used in wet recipes like beverages, icings, and sauces. Stevia granules can be used for baking.

**Xylitol**
Studies have now shown that xylitol has anti-candida yeast properties. Xylitol is also a popular sweetener and works well in any recipe; it is also great for baked goods. Yeast cannot properly metabolize xylitol, so do not be concerned that it is feeding your health problems; it may be eliminating them! I opt for birch bark xylitol over corncob xylitol.

**Manuka Honey and Pure Maple Syrup**
These are Kaufmann 2 sweeteners. In some recipes, com-

bine honey and stevia to get the right consistency and flavor. Manuka honey adds a depth of richness to any recipe, but it does not have to be the only sweet agent.

With any sweetener, always err on the side of not enough rather than too much. For example, if you are converting a recipe that calls for 1 cup of sugar, only use 1/4 a cup of xylitol, and adjust to taste.

## Oils

Some of the common oils many are accustom to cooking with are likely not permitted on The Kaufmann Diets, such as corn or canola oil. Below is a list of Kaufmann Diet–friendly oils and a guideline for cooking with them.

### Olive Oil

Not only does olive oil have anti-fungal properties, but it is also a great all-purpose oil for sautéing, salad dressings, marinades, and dipping. Olive oil is not recommended for high temperature frying.

### Coconut Oil

Coconut oil has several anti-fungal components. Coconut oil is good for high heat frying and sautéing. It is also great for baking, but because coconut oil solidifies at cooler temperatures, you may have to warm the oil slightly by putting the jar in warm water to get an accurate measurement. Do not microwave coconut oil!

### Grapeseed Oil

Grapeseed oil is good for all types of cooking but must be kept in the refrigerator after opening.

### Avocado Oil

Avocado oil has a mild flavor and is a good all-purpose oil.

### Sesame Oil

Sesame oil is a flavoring oil for salads and marinades. It is not recommended for cooking and must be refrigerated.

## Kaufmann Conversions of Old Favorites

Do you miss mom's fabulous Sunday dinners? You can easily convert old favorites to your new Kaufmann lifestyle.

First up is pot roast. Kaufmann 2 allows sweet potatoes, which can be used in a lot of recipes as a substitution for white potatoes. Cook your favorite pot roast, but use sweet potatoes. Sweet potatoes take a little less time to cook, so just add them during the last 45 minutes of cooking.

For the gravy, mix 1 tablespoon of tapioca flour with 1/2 cup of water to make a slurry, and mix into pan drippings.

Add sweet potatoes to your vegetable soup recipe, or substitute sweet potatoes for white potatoes in potato salad. Let your imagination run wild!

How about a fried chicken dinner? Brown rice flour is excellent for frying chicken or even fish. It is light and crisps well when used as a breading.

Cold winter days just scream for a chicken pot pie. Use arrowroot flour as a substitute in your crust. Thicken the gravy using chicken stock and tapioca flour, and then add Kaufmann Diet–friendly veggies and chicken.

Spaghetti and meatballs a childhood favorite? Make your meatballs Kaufmann Diet–friendly by using cooked quinoa or quinoa flakes instead of bread/bread crumbs for the filler. You can use a canned tomato sauce that does not have sugar or corn sweetener, and try spaghetti squash (Kaufmann 1) or lentil pasta (Kaufmann 2) for noodles.

Cauliflower is another multi-purpose gem when on The Kaufmann Diet. This versatile vegetable can be steamed, mashed, or baked. Cauliflower also accepts other flavors well for seasoning, like garlic and fresh herbs. Mashed cauliflower with butter and salt tastes similar to mashed potatoes. Riced cauliflower can substitute for rice in fried rice recipes. When steamed, liquid drained and squeezed out, cauliflower can make a great base for mock potato pancakes and pizza crust.

The Kaufmann Diet can and will open your eyes to a whole new world of possibilities. Do not get discouraged with what you see as restrictions, but rather embrace the endless possibilities of foods that will dramatically change and enhance your life.

### Crackers and Pastas

You can have certain crackers and pasta while following the Kaufmann 2 Diet but beware; do not be fooled by gluten-free labels. So many new cracker and pasta selections are now on the shelves, but not all are Kaufmann Diet–friendly. The term gluten–free might mean no wheat was used, but it can mean that there are other ingredients added that are not allowed, like corn, sugar, or potato starch. Yes, both corn and sugar are gluten free! When you find a box of crackers or pasta that looks tempting, read all of the ingredients before you buy. There are many varieties of crackers and pasta that are perfectly acceptable, but you have to look closely.

# CHAPTER 3

# Breakfast

Many people cannot imagine life without breakfast, but much of what constitutes breakfast food is off limits on The Kaufmann Diets. That said, there is never a reason to feel deprived while on The Kaufmann Diet, especially for your first meal of the day. Since you are skipping the cereal, toast, and bagels, here are plenty of recipes to help you start your day off on the right foot. These are healthy, satisfying, and all on The Kaufmann Diet.

# Amaranth Pancakes

*(Kaufmann 1)*

*Makes about 12 (4") pancakes*

## Ingredients:

2 large eggs
½ cup almond milk
2 tsp oil
½ cup amaranth flour
½ cup tapioca flour
⅓ cup arrowroot starch
½ tsp cinnamon *(optional)*
2 tsp baking powder
¼ tsp salt

## Directions:

Beat eggs in a medium to large bowl, stir in almond milk and oil.

Mix the remaining dry ingredients in a separate bowl with a wire whisk.

Stir the wet ingredients into the dry ingredients with a spoon or spatula until just combined.

Heat a lightly greased griddle or skillet to medium high and cook until bubbly. Flip and cook until done.

Serve with fresh berries (Kaufmann 1) or honey or maple syrup (Kaufmann 2).

# Egg Muffins with Bacon, Spinach & Goat Cheese

*(Kaufmann 2, remove goat cheese to make Kaufmann 1)*

*by Lindsey Crouch*

*6 Servings*

## Ingredients:

12 eggs
¼ cup almond milk
½ tsp salt
¼ tsp pepper
2 cups spinach *(chopped)*
4 bacon slices
*(cooked, drained and chopped)*
½ cup goat cheese

## Directions:

Preheat oven to 350°. Use a regular 12 cup muffin pan. Spray the muffin pan with non-stick cooking spray.

In a large bowl, beat eggs. Add milk, salt and pepper and beat again. Stir in the rest of the ingredients. Fill each muffin cups with egg mixture about ¾ full.

Bake for 25 minutes. Remove from the oven, let the muffins cool for 10 to 15 minutes before removing them from the pan.

# Oatmeal Mason Jars

*(Kaufmann 2)*

*Makes 1 Jar*

## Ingredients:

½ cup uncooked quick oats
1 pinch salt
⅛ tsp cinnamon
*(or any spice you like)*
1 to 2 Tbsp dried unsweetened fruit *(cranberries, strawberries or blueberries)*
1 to 2 Tbsp almonds, pecans or cashews

## Directions:

To make your oatmeal jar, layer oatmeal, salt, spice, fruit and nuts.

Make as many as you like and store in a dry area.

Mix it up and have fun with it. Be mindful of the fruits and nuts you use, keeping them Kaufmann 1 and Kaufmann 2 will be better for you.

### To Cook:

Pour ¾ cup of boiling water over oatmeal and stir. Be careful—the jar will be hot.

Let stand for 4 to 5 minutes then enjoy.

# Quinoa Hot Breakfast Cereal

*(Kaufmann 1)*

*by Abby Miller*

*1 Serving*

## Ingredients:

⅓ cup quinoa *(uncooked, rinsed and drained)*
⅔ cup water
¼ cup *(or more)* coconut milk
2 Tbsp flax meal *(or ground flax seed)*
1 tsp cinnamon *(to taste)*
1 Tbsp stevia or xylitol *(to taste)*
1 Tbsp almond butter

Optional nuts and fruits: almonds, walnuts, pecans, strawberries, blueberries and green apple cut into small chunks.

## Directions:

Combine quinoa and water in a saucepan and bring to boil. Turn down to a low simmer and cook until quinoa is soft, about 10 min. Make sure there is still a little liquid in the mixture. If all the liquid has cooked out, you can add more water. Stir in coconut milk and heat through.

Remove from heat and stir in flax meal, cinnamon, sweetener, and almond butter. (The flax will absorb the extra liquid and make a thick, oatmeal like consistency.)

Serve in a bowl and garnish with your favorite Kaufmann 1 approved nuts and fruit.

# Sweet Potato Hash Bowl

*(Kaufmann 2)*

*2 Servings*

## Ingredients:

1 to 2 Tbsp extra virgin olive oil
1 large sweet potato *(diced)*
½ small onion *(diced)*
4 eggs
salt and pepper *(to taste)*
¼ cup salsa
1 avocado *(sliced or diced)*
fresh cilantro

## Directions:

Heat olive oil in a skillet over medium to medium high heat. Sauté sweet potato and onion until caramelized and slightly crispy or until desired texture. Season with salt and pepper. Remove from pan and set aside.

Scramble eggs in a bowl and season with salt and pepper. Put a little more olive oil in skillet then scramble eggs. Add the fried potatoes and onions and toss in with the eggs. You can add the salsa now or pour it over the eggs when served.

Serve in bowls topped with avocado, cilantro, and more salsa.

## CHAPTER 4

# Drinks & Smoothies

On The Kaufmann Diets, you are encouraged to drink plenty of pure water. This is important for overall health and well-being, but it is not to say that there are not other healthy beverages available to you on The Kaufmann Diets. Whether you are looking for something refreshing or something to sate your appetite, all of these drinks and smoothies are Kaufmann Diet approved.

# Berry, Mint and Lime Smoothie

*(Kaufmann 1)*

*1 Serving*

## Ingredients:

¾ cup almond milk
¾ cup frozen blackberries or blueberries
¼ cup mint leaves
2 Tbsp lime juice
1 Tbsp chia seeds
pinch of salt

## Directions:

Put all the ingredients in a blender with a ½ cup ice and blend until smooth.

# Golden Milk

*(Kaufmann 1 or 2)*

*1 Serving*

## Ingredients:

1 cup coconut, almond or hemp milk
½ tsp turmeric
½ tsp ground ginger
¼ tsp ground cardamon
pinch of stevia *(or 1 tsp honey – Kaufmann 2)*

## Directions:

Combine all the ingredients in a drinking glass and stir. You could also put in a blender to make a little frothy.

# Iced Turmeric Latte

*(Kaufmann 1)*

*1 Serving*

## Ingredients:

1 cup cashew milk
4 tsp grated fresh turmeric
1 tsp grated fresh ginger
1 tsp fresh lemon juice
¼ tsp ground cardamon
pinch of salt
stevia to taste

## Directions:

Whisk all ingredients together in a bowl and let sit about 5 to 10 minutes so flavors can meld together.

Strain with a fine mesh sieve then pour over ice.

# Liver Detox Green Smoothie

*(Kaufmann 1)*

*by Melissa Henig*

*1 Serving*

## Ingredients:

1 handful spinach
½ cucumber
*(peeled and cut in half)*
10 raw almonds
2 Tbsp fresh parsley
1" ginger root
1 small green apple *(cut in quarters)*
2 tsp hemp seeds
1 Tbsp raw coconut oil
1 cup filtered water

## Directions:

Put all the ingredients in a blender and blend until smooth.

# No Sugar Green Smoothie

*(Kaufmann 1)*

*by Melissa Henig*

*1 Serving*

## Ingredients:

1 avocado *(pitted and cut in half)*
½ cucumber
*(peeled and cut in half)*
1 handful spinach
juice of 1 lemon
1 cup filtered water

## Directions:

Put all the ingredients in a blender and blend until smooth.

# CHAPTER 5

# Snacks & Appetizers

For many, snacking between meals is a must in order to stay satisfied. Other people enjoy priming their tastebuds for a delicious meal with an equally delicious appetizer. Whether you are entertaining a crowd, or just feeling peckish, here you will find a variety of snacks and appetizers that are sure to both satisfy your tastebuds and keep you on The Kaufmann Diets.

# Artichoke & Spinach Dip

*(Kaufmann 2)*

*by Lindsey Crouch*

## Ingredients:

1 tsp extra virgin olive oil
1 can artichoke hearts *(packed in water) (drained and chopped)*
2 cups spinach *(chopped)*
8 oz cream cheese
½ cup plain Greek yogurt
½ tsp crushed red pepper flakes
⅛ tsp garlic powder
¼ tsp salt
dash of fresh ground pepper

## Directions:

Put olive oil in a skillet and heat over medium to medium high heat. Add artichoke and spinach and sauté until spinach is wilted and artichoke is heated through.

Lower the heat and add the rest of the ingredients, cream cheese, yogurt, pepper flakes, garlic powder, salt, and pepper.

Stir to combine until cheese melts and dip is heated through.

# Avocado Butter

*(Kaufmann 1)*

*Makes 1 Cup*

## Ingredients:

½ cup butter *(softened)*
½ cup mashed avocado
3 Tbsp fresh lime juice
2 Tbsp minced Italian parsley
2 garlic cloves *(minced)*
salt to taste

## Directions:

In a bowl, mash the butter and avocado together with a potato masher. Add the rest of the ingredients and mix until combined. Cover and chill.

Serve with Flat Bread. Recipe in this section.

# Avocado Deviled Eggs

*(Kaufmann 1)*

*6 Servings*

## Ingredients:

6 large eggs *(hard boiled)*
1 avocado *(halved, seeded and peeled)*
2 Tbsp diced red onion
2 Tbsp chopped cilantro
1 Tbsp lime juice
salt and pepper *(to taste)*

**Garnish Options:** lime zest, cayenne pepper, chopped chives, crumbled bacon

## Directions:

Peel hardboiled eggs and cut in half lengthwise. Carefully remove yolks and put in a mixing bowl. Set egg white halves aside on serving plate.

Put the avocado, red onion, cilantro, lime juice, salt, and pepper in the bowl with the yolks and mash and mix with a fork until desired consistency.

With a spoon or pastry bag, fill the egg white halves with the egg yolk/avocado mixture.

Garnish with your favorite toppings.

# Bread & Butter Pickles

*(Kaufmann 1)*

*by Joy Miller*

*Makes a 1 Quart Jar*

## Ingredients:

2 tsp coarse salt
1 tsp mustard seed
1 tsp pickling spice
¼ tsp celery seed
2 to 4 pickling cucumbers or 1 English cucumber *(thinly sliced)*
1 onion *(thinly sliced)*
½ cup apple cider vinegar
¼ cup stevia granules *(not liquid stevia)*
generous pinch of red pepper flakes *(optional)*

## Directions:

Place all dry spices in bottom of a 1 quart mason jar.

Layer pickles and onion to the top.

Mix vinegar and stevia and pour over cucumber and onion slices. If the liquid doesn't cover all of the cucumbers, either mix a little more of the vinegar and stevia mixture or if just a little space not covered, add water to cover.

Secure top and shake to distribute spices. Place in refrigerator for 7 days, shaking jar twice a day.

Pickles will keep up to 4 months in refrigerator.

# Cinnamon Roasted Almonds

*(Kaufmann 1)*

*Makes 4 Cups*

## Ingredients:

1 egg white
1 tsp cold water
4 cups whole almonds
¼ cup stevia
¼ tsp salt
½ tsp ground cinnamon

## Directions:

Preheat oven to 250°F.

In a large bowl beat the egg white with a whisk. Add the water and whisk until frothy, but not stiff. Add the almonds and stir.

In a small bowl mix the stevia, salt, and cinnamon together then sprinkle over almonds and toss to coat.

Spread almonds out on a large rimmed baking sheet. Bake for 1 hour, stirring every 15 minutes, until golden.

Let cool completely and store in an airtight container.

# Crispy Baked Chicken Wings

*(Kaufmann 1)*

*4 Servings*

## Ingredients:

2 lbs chicken wings
*(tips removed, drumettes and flats separated)*
2 Tbsp extra virgin olive oil
salt and pepper to taste
favorite spices
favorite chopped herbs for garnish

## Directions:

Preheat oven to 450°F.

Line a large baking sheet with parchment paper. You might have to work with 2 baking sheets.

In a large bowl, toss the wings with olive oil, salt and pepper.

Sprinkle on your favorite spices and toss again.

Arrange wings on baking sheet in a single layer without touching each other.

Bake in oven for 30 minutes, remove from oven, flip wings over and bake for another 10 to 15 minutes.

Put in a big bowl and serve warm topped with your favorite chopped herbs for garnish.

# Deviled Eggs

*(Kaufmann 1)*

*Makes 12*

## Ingredients:

6 eggs *(hard boiled)*
2 tsp dry mustard
2 Tbsp plain yogurt
salt and pepper to taste
paprika for garnish

## Directions:

Peel the eggs and cut in half lengthwise. Separate the yolks from the whites. Put the yolks into a bowl and put the whites aside.

Add the mustard, yogurt, salt, and pepper to the yolks and mash with a fork. Spoon the mixture into the egg whites and garnish with paprika.

# Everyday Bread

*(Kaufmann 1)*

*by Jordan Palmer*

## Ingredients:

2 cups blanched almond flour
¾ cup arrowroot flour
¼ cup flax seed meal
½ tsp baking soda
1 tsp xylitol *(optional)*
1 tsp sea salt
3 large eggs
⅓ cup plain yogurt
1 tsp apple cider vinegar
2 Tbsp avocado oil *(or other Kaufmann approved cooking oil)*

## Directions:

Preheat oven to 350°F.

In a large bowl add the almond flour, arrowroot, flax seed meal, baking soda, xylitol, and salt and sift together with a wire whisk until combined.

In another bowl add the eggs, yogurt, apple cider vinegar, and oil and beat with a whisk until combined and frothy.

Pour wet ingredients into the dry ingredients and mix well.

**Thin Sandwich Bread:**
Pour the mixture onto a parchment or Silpat lined 13x18" rimmed baking sheet and spread evenly leaving a ¼" gap from the edge or if spreading batter to the edge, make sure to grease the edges of the pan. Bake for 8 to 10 minutes or until a toothpick inserted into the center comes out clean. Cut into sandwich sized squares.

**Dinner Bread:**
Pour the mixture into a well greased 9x9" baking pan, spread evenly. Bake for 20 to 24 minutes or until a toothpick inserted into the center comes out clean. Cut into 9 squares.

# Flat Bread

*(Kaufmann 1)*

*Makes about 6 Servings*

## Ingredients:

½ cup almond flour
½ cup tapioca flour
1 cup coconut milk *(full fat)*
pinch of salt

## Directions:

Mix all the ingredients in a bowl.

Heat a non-stick skillet over medium heat. Pour about ¼ cup of the batter (more for larger serving) into the hot skillet.

Once the batter fluffs up and looks firm, flip it over and cook until done.

Serve with your favorite recipe or warm with butter.

# Holiday Green Dip with Veggie Sticks

*(Kaufmann 2)*

*by Joy Miller*

*Makes about 2 cups of Dip*

## Ingredients:

**Dip:**

⅓ cup fresh parsley leaves
⅓ cup fresh dill fronds
⅓ cup fresh tarragon leaves
⅓ cup fresh chives
1 garlic clove
*(smashed and peeled)*
juice of half a lemon
2 Tbsp mayonnaise
½ cup Greek yogurt
½ cup sour cream
⅓ cup goat cheese
salt and pepper to taste

**Veggies:**

green beans *(blanched)*
carrots *(cut into sticks)*
red bell pepper strips
green onions
cucumber *(cut into sticks)*
cherry tomatoes *(on toothpicks)*

Be creative and use any veggies you like.

## Directions:

Rinse the herbs and dry in a salad spinner. Put in a food processor and pulse until minced.

Add garlic, lemon juice, mayonnaise, yogurt, sour cream, and goat cheese to processor and pulse until blended well, scraping down sides of processor bowl as you go.

Salt and pepper to taste.

Serve in cups. Spoon dip into the bottom of the cup and put an assortment of veggies into the cup.

Great to have set out at parties.

# Hummus

*(Kaufmann 2)*

*Makes about 3 Cups*

## Ingredients:

2 (15 oz) cans chickpeas *(drained & rinsed)*
2 to 4 garlic cloves *(smashed)*
⅔ cup tahini
⅓ cup lemon juice *(about 2 lemons)*
¼ cup extra virgin olive oil
1 ¼ tsp coarse salt
⅛ to ¼ tsp cayenne pepper
¼ to ½ cup water *(depending on consistency)*

## Directions:

Put all ingredients (except water) into a food processor and blend until smooth.

While still processing, add some of the water, a little at a time, until desired consistency.

Serve in bowl and drizzle with extra virgin olive oil.

# Hummus with Turmeric

*(Kaufmann 2)*

*Makes about 3 Cups*

## Ingredients:

2 (15 oz) cans chickpeas *(drained & rinsed)*
2 to 4 garlic cloves *(smashed)*
Juice of 1 lemon
3 Tbsp tahini
⅔ cup extra virgin olive oil
½ tsp coarse salt
2 tsp turmeric powder
½ tsp cumin
⅛ tsp cayenne pepper *(add more for a little heat)*
1 Tbsp apple cider vinegar
¼ to ½ cup water *(depending on consistency)*

## Directions:

Put all ingredients (except water) into a food processor and blend until smooth.

While still processing, add some of the water, a little at a time, until desired consistency.

Serve in bowl and drizzle with extra virgin olive oil.

# Not Cornbread

*(Kaufmann 2)*

*by Joy Miller*

*9 Servings*

## Ingredients:

½ cup almond flour
¼ cup coconut flour
½ tsp coarse salt
½ tsp baking soda
3 large eggs
2 Tbsp butter *(melted)*
2 Tbsp coconut oil *(melted)*
2 Tbsp honey
½ cup unsweetened almond milk

## Directions:

Preheat oven to 325°F.

Grease a 8x8" baking pan with butter.

Mix all the dry ingredients in a large bowl and all the wet ingredients in a separate medium bowl, beating with a fork to break up eggs and mixing well.

Add the wet ingredients to the dry ingredients and mix with a spoon or spatula until just combined.

Pour the batter into the prepared baking pan and bake for 25 to 30 minutes, or until a toothpick inserted in the center of the bread comes out clean.

# Pecan Bites

*(Kaufmann 2)*

*by Jordan Palmer*

*12 Servings*

## Ingredients:

2 Tbsp butter
2 Tbsp coconut oil
2 cups chopped pecans
1 cup sliced almonds
¼ cup flax seed meal
¼ cup honey
1 tsp cinnamon
½ tsp salt
1 tsp vanilla
½ tsp liquid stevia

## Directions:

Put butter and coconut oil in a skillet and melt over medium heat.

Add pecans and almonds. Stir to coat. Add the remaining ingredients and stir constantly for 5 to 8 minutes until the nuts become crunchy. Feel free to cook a little longer for a crunchier bar, just be careful not to let them burn.

Remove from heat and spoon mixture into 12 muffin cups (don't use paper liners) and press firmly with back of spoon.

Put in freezer for 1 to 2 hours.

Loosen rounds from muffin tin with a narrow spatula or plastic knife. They should pop right out.

**Tip:** After you have cooked the ingredients you can also add your favorite dried fruit like shredded coconut or dried cranberries.

# Simple Roasted Pecans

*(Kaufmann 1)*

*Makes 2 Cups*

## Ingredients:

2 Tbsp melted butter
2 cups pecan halves
salt to taste
*(or any other seasoning)*

## Directions:

Preheat oven to 250°F.

Toss the pecans with the melted butter and salt.

Spread pecans out on a large rimmed baking sheet. Bake for about 40 to 45 minutes, stirring every 10 minutes, until fragrant. Watch carefully, pecans tend to burn easily.

Let cool completely and store in an airtight container.

# Stuffed Jalapeños

*(Kaufmann 2)*

*by Lindsey Crouch*

*20 Servings*

## Ingredients:

10 whole fresh jalapeños *(2" to 3" in size)*
8 oz pack cream cheese *(softened)*
garlic powder *(to taste)*
Cajun seasoning *(to taste)*
10 slices turkey bacon *(cut in half crosswise)*

## Directions:

Preheat oven to 375°F.

Cut jalapeños in half, length wise, and remove seeds and membranes. Be careful not to touch your eyes after handling jalapeños.

In a bowl, mix cream cheese, garlic powder, and Cajun seasoning. You can get creative and mix other spices with the cream cheese.

Spread cream cheese mixture into jalapeño halves. Wrap each jalapeño with half slice of turkey bacon. Pierce with toothpick if you can't get the bacon to hold properly.

Place wrapped jalapeños on parchment lined baking sheet and cook for about 20 to 25 minutes. You can turn broiler on at end to crisp. Be careful that you don't burn the toothpicks.

# Thyme Roasted Nuts

*(Kaufmann 1)*

## Ingredients:

2 cups walnuts, almonds or pecans *(or a mixture)*
1 Tbsp chopped fresh thyme
2 Tbsp extra virgin olive oil
½ tsp coarse salt

## Directions:

Preheat oven to 350°F.

Toss all the ingredients together in a bowl until the nuts are evenly coated with oil and seasonings.

Spread the nuts out onto a rimmed baking sheet in a single layer and roast in the oven until golden and fragrant, about 10 to 15 minutes, stirring nuts half way through.

Store in an airtight container.

# CHAPTER 6

# Salad Dressings & Sauces

Most salad dressings and sauces that you will find at a restaurant or at the grocery store likely contain ingredients that many would seek to avoid. Often these are loaded with sugar, vinegar, corn syrup, lots of sodium, and preservatives. Often though, many people feel deprived if they must give up salad dressings and sauces altogether. So, we have created a solution. These recipes for salad dressings and sauces will make you feel like you never gave anything up to begin with.

# Avocado Cashew Dressing

*(Kaufmann 1)*

## Ingredients:

½ cup raw unsalted cashews
2 garlic cloves
½ avocado
*(pitted, peeled and diced)*
½ cup unsweetened coconut milk
1 tsp dried dill
1 tsp dried chives
⅛ tsp cayenne pepper
1 tsp lime juice
salt to taste
½ cup water *(more or less for desired consistency)*

## Directions:

Soak cashews covered in water for 6 hours to overnight. Drain.

With blender or food processor running, drop garlic cloves in feed tube or hole in lid to chop.

Turn off blender then add the remaining ingredients and about a third of the water. Process until smooth adding more water for desired consistency.

Put in a jar and let sit in refrigerator for a fews hours to let flavors meld.

**Tip:** If you are in a hurry you can boil the cashews in water for 10 minutes, drain and let cool.

# Creamy Avocado Lime Dressing

*(Kaufmann 1)*

## Ingredients:

¼ cup lime juice *(about 2 limes)*
1 Tbsp extra virgin olive oil
1 Tbsp water *(or more)*
½ of a medium to large avocado
¼ cup lightly packed fresh cilantro
1 small to medium jalapeño *(seeded, deribbed and roughly chopped)*
1 garlic clove *(roughly chopped)*
¼ tsp salt

## Directions:

In a small food processor or blender, add all the ingredients and process until smooth.

# Cucumber Yogurt Dressing

*(Kaufmann 1)*

## Ingredients:

2 cups plain yogurt
1 medium cucumber *(peeled and grated)*
1 garlic clove *(minced)*
juice of ½ lemon
salt to taste

## Directions:

Mix all the ingredients together and put in an airtight container. Let sit in refrigerator for at least 2 hours for flavors to meld.

# Ketchup

*(Kaufmann 1)*

*Makes about 1 Cup*

## Ingredients:

1 can tomato paste
¼ cup water
1 Tbsp apple cider vinegar
4 drops liquid Stevia
*(or sweetened to taste)*
½ tsp sea salt
½ tsp cumin
¼ tsp mustard powder
½ tsp cinnamon
⅛ tsp ground cloves
¼ tsp onion powder

## Directions:

Mix all the ingredients together in a medium saucepan and simmer over medium heat, stirring constantly, for about 5 to 10 minutes.

If it is too thick, thin with small amounts (1 Tbsp) of water at a time

Store in a airtight container in the refrigerator for up to a week.

# Lemon Vinaigrette

*(Kaufmann 1)*

## Ingredients:

¼ cup fresh squeezed lemon juice *(about 2 lemons)*
½ cup extra virgin olive oil
coarse salt and fresh ground pepper to taste

## Directions:

Put lemon juice in bowl, start whisking. As you are whisking, slowly pour olive oil into bowl in a steady stream. Season with salt and pepper.

# Maple Garlic Marinade

*(Kaufmann 2)*

This simple marinade is great with fish, chicken and pork.

## Ingredients:

¼ cup maple syrup
2 Tbsp coconut aminos
1 garlic clove *(minced)*

## Directions:

In a small bowl, mix maple syrup, coconut aminos and garlic.

Place meat in a baking dish, season with salt and pepper and pour sauce over top. Cover with plastic wrap and marinate in the refrigerator for 30 minutes.

Grill or bake meat until desired doneness.

# Maple Pecan Glaze Drizzle

*(Kaufmann 2)*

This drizzle is great with sliced green apples or drizzle over yogurt or sweet potatoes.

## Ingredients:

¾ cup pecans
¼ cup pure maple syrup
2 Tbsp coconut oil
1 tsp vanilla extract
¼ tsp salt

## Directions:

Put all the ingredients in a blender and blend until smooth.

Store sauce in refrigerator to thicken.

# Mayonnaise

*(Kaufmann 1)*

Use an immersion blender and a tall mason jar.

## Ingredients:

2 egg yolks*
*(room temperature)*
2 tsp fresh lemon juice
½ tsp dry mustard
1 or 2 pinches of salt
1 cup oil
*(avocado, safflower, or light olive)*

## Directions:

Put egg yolks, lemon juice, mustard, and salt into the jar. Pour in a couple of tablespoons of the oil and start to blend. As the mixture thickens, pour in a couple more table spoons of the oil and blend again. Keep alternating pouring and mixing until all the oil has been poured in and the mixture has thickened.

Do not over mix or the mayonnaise will break down.

You can also use a blender putting all the ingredients and a little oil in the blender, turning it on and slowly drizzle the rest of the oil in through the lid.

Store in refrigerator for up to 1 week.

***CONTAINS RAW EGGS:** Take caution when consuming raw and lightly cooked eggs due to the slight risk of salmonella or other food-borne illness. To reduce this risk, we recommend you use only fresh, properly refrigerated, clean grade A or AA eggs with intact shells, and avoid contact between the yolks or whites and the shell. For recipes that call for eggs that are raw or undercooked when the dish is served, use shell eggs that have been treated to destroy salmonella by pasteurization or another approved method.

# Spicy Mustard

*(Kaufmann 1)*

*Makes about 1 Cup*

## Ingredients:

¼ cup yellow *(or a mix of yellow and brown seeds)*
⅓ cup apple cider vinegar
½ cup water
¼ tsp onion powder
¼ tsp garlic powder
¼ tsp turmeric
Pinch of salt *(optional)*
4 to 5 drops stevia *(optional)*

## Directions:

Put the mustard seeds, vinegar and water in a glass jar, stir. Cover with the lid and let sit at room temperature for 24 hours.

Put the mixture and the onion powder, garlic powder and turmeric in a small food processor or blender and blend until desired texture.

Stir in optional salt and/or stevia if desired.

Store in a glass jar with a lid in the refrigerator.

**Note:** Make this your own. Add or remove and adjust spices to your liking. Try different amounts of liquids for a thinner or thicker mustard.

# CHAPTER 7

# Salads

Salads are a staple for the healthy. There are few better ways to get so much nutrition in a single meal. Just because salads are healthy, though, does not mean they cannot be satisfying and delicious. Here are some fresh salad ideas that will put a new spin on a healthy staple.

# Beet, Carrot and Apple Slaw

*(Kaufmann 1)*

*6 Servings*

## Ingredients:

2 large raw beets *(peeled)*
2 large carrots *(peeled)*
2 green apples *(cored and peeled)*
½ cup walnuts
2 lemons *(zest and juice)*
1 Tbsp extra virgin olive oil
salt and pepper to taste
1 Tbsp stevia
*(or honey, Kaufmann 2)*

## Directions

Grate the beets, carrots, and apples with a box grater (large holes) or food processor (you can also cut everything into matchsticks) and put into a large bowl.

Add the walnuts.

Zest the lemons into the bowl then cut in half and squeeze the juice into the bowl also.

Add the oil, salt, pepper, and stevia. If using honey, remember that is Kaufmann 2.

Toss until combined and enjoy.

# Cauliflower (Potato) Salad

*(Kaufmann 1)*

*by Joy Miller*

*8 to 10 Servings*

## Ingredients:

1 head cauliflower
1 cup diced celery
½ cup diced onion
2 hard boiled eggs *(chopped)*
1 cup mayonnaise
2 Tbsp Dijon mustard
*(made with apple cider vinegar)*

**Optional Additions:** chopped bread & butter pickles (recipe in "Snacks & Appetizers" section), ½ cup diced green or red pepper, fresh herbs, celery seed, Old Bay Seasoning, Cajun seasonings, crumbled cooked bacon.

## Directions:

Separate cauliflower into florets and steam until crisp tender, about 10 to 15 minutes. Drain then immediately plunge into ice water bath to cool, drain.

Coarsely chop and put in a large mixing bowl with the rest of the ingredients. Mix then cover and put in the refrigerator for 3 to 4 hours to chill and let the flavors to develop.

**Note:** Add any optional Kaufmann 1 ingredients listed above or any other additions that you like, as long as they are Kaufmann friendly.

# Cranberry Chicken Salad on Green Apple Slices

*(Kaufmann 2)*

*by Joy Miller*

*3 to 4 Servings*

## Ingredients:

2 cooked chicken breast halves *(shredded or chopped)*
½ cup dried unsweetened cranberries
⅓ cup roasted pecans *(chopped)*
⅓ cup celery *(chopped)*
⅓ cup mayonnaise
⅓ cup sour cream
1 Tbsp fresh lemon juice
½ tsp curry powder
salt and pepper to taste
2 to 3 medium green apples *(sliced into rounds)*

## Directions:

Mix all ingredients together except apples in a large bowl.

Spoon onto apple slices and serve.

# Doug's Favorite Meal

*(Kaufmann 1)*

*2 Servings*

## Ingredients:

1 tomato *(diced)*
1 small onion *(diced)*
1 cucumber *(diced)*
1 avocado, *(diced)*
½ cup black olives *(diced)*
3 hard boiled eggs *(sliced)*
smoked salmon or cubes of beef summer sausage
extra virgin olive oil
5 Tbsp freshly squeezed lemon juice

## Directions:

Combine first six ingredients, add sliced boiled eggs and smoked salmon. Top with olive oil and freshly squeezed lemon juice.

**Note:** This meal is quick and easy to prepare, and tastes great! You can switch it up to your liking by adding in your favorite protein, veggies, nuts, or quinoa.

This quick and easy dish is Doug Kaufmann's favorite.

# Honey Lime Quinoa Fruit Salad

*(Kaufmann 2)*

*4 Servings*

## Ingredients:

1 cup uncooked quinoa
1 ½ cup strawberries *(sliced)*
1 cup blackberries
1 cup blueberries
1 mango *(peeled and diced)*
2 Tbsp chopped basil
¼ cup honey
2 Tbsp lime juice

## Directions:

Cook quinoa per directions on package and let cool.

In a large bowl toss the cooked quinoa, fruit, and basil.

Combine honey and lime juice in a small bowl. Pour over the mixed fruit and lightly toss.

# Kale & Brussels Sprouts Salad

*(Kaufmann 2)*

*by Lindsey Crouch*

*6 to 8 Servings*

## Ingredients:

**Salad:**

10 to 12 oz Brussels sprouts *(shaved/shredded)*
10 oz bag julienne cut broccoli slaw
2 packed cups kale *(finely chopped and stems removed)*
4 green onions *(chopped)*
1 cup cilantro *(chopped)*
1 cucumber *(peeled and diced)*
1 cup artichoke hearts *(chopped)*
1 cup pecans *(chopped)*
1 cup unsweetened dried cranberries
1 large avocado *(diced)*
½ lemon

**Dressing:**

⅓ cup hemp oil *(extra virgin olive oil will work too)*
2 Tbsp apple cider vinegar
2 Tbsp honey
salt and pepper to taste

## Directions:

Cut stems and discard coarse outer leaves of Brussels sprouts, then shave thinly with a chef's knife or you can find some that are pre shredded. Put shaved Brussels sprouts in a large salad bowl. Add bag of broccoli slaw to bowl. Add finely chopped kale leaves, green onions, cilantro, cucumber, artichoke hearts, pecans and cranberries. Toss. Add avocado. Squeeze in lemon juice. Toss again gently.

In a large liquid measuring cup, add hemp oil, apple cider vinegar, honey and salt and pepper. Stir with whisk or fork until combined. Drizzle over salad and toss until coated throughout. Serve right away.

# KTC 10 Layered Salad

*(Kaufmann 2)*

*6 to 8 Servings*

## Ingredients:

**Salad:**

1 small head iceberg lettuce *(chopped)*
4 tomatoes *(cut into wedges)*
1 cucumber *(chopped or sliced)*
5 oz baby spinach
½ red onion *(quartered and thinly sliced)*
8 hard boiled eggs *(chopped)*
salt and pepper to taste
1 lb bacon *(cooked and chopped)*
4 green onions *(thinly sliced)*
4 oz crumbled goat cheese
10 oz bag frozen green peas *(thawed)*
Fresh chopped dill *(or dried)*

**Dressing:**

¾ cup mayonnaise
¾ cup sour cream
1 ½ tsp xylitol

## Directions:

Layer the salad ingredients in a clear glass bowl for presentation. Put a good layer of lettuce on the bottom, then tomato, cucumber, spinach, onion, and eggs. Season egg layer with salt and pepper. Layer the bacon, green onion, cheese, and peas.

Mix the mayonnaise, sour cream and xylitol in a small bowl and spread over the top of the salad. Garnish with dill. Cover and keep refrigerated until served.

# Mason Jar Salads

*(Kaufmann 1)*

We have seen these on the internet and thought it was a great way to make some salads for on the go ahead of time and make them Kaufmann 1 friendly.

You can make these salads anyway you like. We like to make them for the work week and just grab one from the fridge when we go to work.

Get some jars, preferably glass with good lids that seal and fill them up.

You can make your favorite dressing and put some in the bottom of the jar or keep it in a separate container. If you put it in the jar, place your harder veggie items in the bottom, they won't get soggy and greens would wilt.

Play around with them and try different vegetables and proteins.

**Start from bottom to top:**

dressing
onion
red, green, yellow or orange bell peppers
diced carrots
cucumbers
grape tomatoes
greens of choice *(stuff them in)*
walnuts
diced chicken *(or your favorite protein)*

**Dressing:** Pour a little of this in each jar or separate containers.

½ cup extra virgin olive oil
3 Tbsp lemon juice
fresh or dried herbs *(thyme, dill, chives, etc.)*
salt and pepper to taste

# Quinoa Tabbouleh

*(Kaufmann 1)*

*6 Servings*

## Ingredients:

1 cup quinoa
2 Tbsp fresh lemon juice
1 garlic clove *(minced)*
½ cup extra virgin olive oil
1 large cucumber *(diced ¼" pieces)*
1 pint cherry or grape tomatoes *(halved)*
⅔ cup chopped Italian parsley
½ cup chopped fresh mint
1 scallions *(thinly sliced)*
salt and pepper

## Directions:

Rinse quinoa in a fine mesh sieve then cook to package instructions. Let cool.

Whisk lemon juice and garlic in a small bowl while slowly adding olive oil. Season with salt and pepper. Set aside.

In a large bowl lightly toss quinoa, cucumber, tomatoes, parsley, mint and scallions. Drizzle with as little or as much of the lemon olive oil dressing as you like. Season with salt and pepper.

Serve at room temp or chilled.

# Salmon Salad

*(Kaufmann 1)*

*by Lindsey Crouch*

*4 Servings*

## Ingredients:

1 lb poached salmon fillet
2 to 3 celery stalks *(diced)*
½ red onion *(thinly sliced)*
½ cucumber *(sliced or diced)*
1 Tbsp salt packed capers *(rinsed and drained)*
1 Tbsp fresh dill
juice of 1 lemon
1 to 2 Tbsp extra virgin olive oil
salt and pepper to taste

## Directions:

In a large bowl combine celery, onion, cucumber, capers and dill. Toss.

In a small bowl whisk the lemon juice and olive oil and pour over salad mix. Toss.

Break salmon into chunk sized pieces and gently fold into salad.

Season with salt and pepper.

# Tuna Salad

*(Kaufmann 1)*

*Makes about 1 ½ Cups*

## Ingredients:

12 oz can tuna
*(best quality packed in water)*
1 small onion *(chopped or sliced)*
1 stalk celery *(diced)*
1 carrot *(diced)*
1 small tomato *(diced)*
1 jalapeño pepper *(diced)*
½ cup plain yogurt
1 Tbsp lemon juice
salt and pepper to taste

## Directions:

Drain tuna then flake into a bowl with a fork. Add all the ingredients and lightly toss.

Serve on a bed of greens or with cucumber slices to dip with.

# Tuna Stuffed Avocados

*(Kaufmann 1)*

*2 to 4 Servings*

## Ingredients:

2 avocados *(halved and pitted)*
1 lime
1 (5 oz) can Solid White Tuna packed in water *(drained)*
2 to 3 Tbsp Greek yogurt
2 to 3 Tbsp red onion *(finely diced)*
½ red bell pepper *(diced)* *(or any color pepper)*
½ tsp dried dill *(or 1 tsp fresh)*
salt and pepper to taste

Garnish with sliced jalapeño and tomatoes.

## Directions:

Splash avocado halves with lime juice.

In a bowl, mix tuna, yogurt, red onion, red pepper, dill, salt and pepper.

Spoon into avocado halves. Garnish with jalapeño slices and tomatoes.

# CHAPTER 8

# Soups

Sometimes, a bowl of soup is just what the doctor ordered. However, a lot of canned soups, or even other seemingly healthy soups you would find at a restaurant or cafe, contain ingredients not permitted on The Kaufmann Diets. Fortunately, making a good bowl of nutritious, Kaufmann Diet-approved soup is easy. Whether you are cooking for a group, or cooking in bulk to enjoy later, everyone is sure to find a soup to love in the following pages.

# Avocado Chicken Soup

*(Kaufmann 1)*

*4 Servings*

## Ingredients:

1 garlic clove
1 jalapeño *(seeds and ribs removed)*
2 avocados *(skinned and pitted)*
1 Tbsp lime juice
¼ to ½ tsp ground red pepper *(to taste)*
1 to 2 Tbsp extra virgin olive oil
1 onion *(diced)*
4 cups chicken broth
1 lb boneless skinless chicken breasts *(cut into ½" strips)*
salt and pepper to taste

## Directions:

In a blender, combine the garlic, jalapeño, avocados, lime juice, ground red pepper, and 1 cup water. Puree until smooth and set aside.

Heat the oil in a 5 qt pot over medium heat. Sauté the onion and cook, stirring frequently, until translucent, about 5 to 6 minutes.

Add the broth, salt and pepper. Bring to a simmer. Stir the chicken into the pot and cook until done, about 15 to 20 minutes.

Add the avocado puree and let heat through.

# Beef Bone Broth (slow cooker)

*(Kaufmann 1)*

*Makes about 5 Cups*

## Ingredients:

3 to 4 lbs beef bone mixture *(short ribs, oxtails, knuckles, neck bones)*
2 medium carrots *(unpeeled and cut into 2" pieces)*
3 stalks celery *(cut into 2" pieces)*
2 medium onions *(quartered)*
1 head of garlic *(halved crosswise)*
2 bay leaves
2 Tbsp apple cider vinegar

## Directions:

Arrange all the ingredients in a 6 quart slow cooker and add enough water (preferably filtered) to cover the ingredients by an inch or two.

Cook on low for about 24 or up to 48 hours. Check occasionally, skimming off any foam on the surface and add additional water to keep the ingredients covered.

The broth is ready when it is dark and flavorful. The bones may crumble after a long time cooking. You will know that you have extracted all the nutrients possible. Not all bones will crumble. Taste it; if it is flavorful and good, it is done.

Strain the broth through a fine mesh strainer to remove all the pieces of bone and vegetables. For a clearer broth, strain again through cheesecloth.

Cool the broth to room temperature and then refrigerate. When it becomes more solid you can skim the fat from the surface and discard.

To serve – spoon into a mug or bowl and warm.

**Optional:** This adds great flavor. Preheat oven to 400°F. Toss the bones with olive oil to coat and place single layer on a baking sheet. Roast for about 1 hour turning once until evenly browned then put into slow cooker.

# Cauliflower Soup

*(Kaufmann 1)*

*by Joy Miller*

*4 Servings*

## Ingredients:

1 lb turkey breakfast sausage
*(or any good sausage you prefer)*
3 Tbsp butter
½ onion *(diced)*
1 large head cauliflower
*(cut in small pieces)*
1 can chicken broth
3 cups water
salt and pepper to taste
8 oz pkg cream cheese
*(room temp, cut into cubes)*

## Directions:

Crumble sausage into a large pot and brown over medium heat until cooked through. Remove from pot and let drain on paper towels.

Remove any grease in the pot left from the sausage. Add butter and sauté onion until translucent, 4 to 5 minutes. Add the cauliflower and stir to coat. Pour in the chicken broth and water and season with salt and pepper. Simmer until cauliflower is soft.

With a slotted spoon, remove about ¾'s of the cauliflower and process in a food processor. Return to the pot along with the sausage.

Add cheese and let melt throughout.

If you need to thicken the soup, you can make a arrowroot powder slurry (1 Tbsp arrowroot powder and ½ cup warm water). Just add a little bit of the mixture until desired thickness.

# Chicken Meatballs & Kale Soup

*(Kaufmann 1)*

*4 Servings*

## Ingredients:

2 Tbsp extra virgin olive oil *(divided)*
2 medium shallots *(minced)*
1 scallion *(all parts minced)* *(more for garnish)*
2 garlic cloves *(minced)*
¼ tsp red pepper flakes
1 lb ground chicken
salt and pepper to taste
1 lemon *(very thinly sliced and seeds removed)* *(more for garnish)*
2 cups chicken broth
1 large bunch curly kale *(destemmed and chopped)*

## Directions:

Heat 1 Tbsp olive oil in a large heavy pot over medium heat. Add shallot, scallion, garlic, and sauté until soft and fragrant.

In a large bowl combine chicken, sautéed mixture, red pepper flakes, salt and pepper to taste.

Shape mixture into 8 to 10 meatballs.

Heat 1 Tbsp olive oil in the pot and cook meatballs until browned on all sides.

Add lemon slices and let cook until slightly browned and soft.

Add chicken broth and bring to a simmer and cover. Simmer until meatballs are cooked through.

Add kale to pot and cook until tender and bright green. Season with salt & pepper.

Serve and garnish with sliced green scallion tops and more lemon slices.

# Pumpkin Turkey Chili (slow cooker)

*(Kaufmann 1)*

*4 to 6 Servings*

## Ingredients:

3 Tbsp extra virgin olive oil *(divided)*
1 onion *(diced)*
½ cup green bell pepper *(diced)*
½ cup yellow bell pepper *(diced)*
1 garlic clove *(minced)*
1 lb. lean ground turkey
1 can (14.5 oz) diced tomatoes
2 cups pumpkin
*(canned or prepared)*
3 cups chicken broth
1 ½ Tbsp chili powder
salt and pepper to taste

### Garnish:

Cilantro

## Directions:

Heat 1 Tbsp olive oil in skillet and sauté onion, peppers, and garlic over medium heat until tender.

Remove from skillet and put in slow cooker.

Add remaining 2 Tbsp olive oil to skillet and cook ground turkey until cooked through and drain.

Add the meat to the sautéed vegetables in the slow cooker. Add tomatoes, pumpkin, chicken broth, chili powder, salt, and pepper and stir.

Cover and cook:
Low for 3 to 4 Hours
High for 2 to 3 Hours

Garnish with cilantro.

# Raw Super Pepper Soup

*(Kaufmann 1)*

*by Melissa Henig*

*2 Servings*

## Ingredients:

1 yellow bell pepper
1 red bell pepper
1 large tomato
1 bunch parsley
1 bunch cilantro
1 bunch basil
½ sweet or yellow onion
½ green apple *(cored)*
½ cup raw almonds
3 Tbsp apple cider vinegar
1" jalapeño
1 tsp Himalayan salt
1 ½ cups filtered water

## Directions:

Rough chop all the ingredients and put in a blender and blend until smooth.

Lightly warm on the stove.

# Roasted Acorn Squash Soup

*(Kaufmann 1)*

*by Lindsey Crouch*

## Ingredients:

2 medium acorn squash *(halved and seeded)*
1 medium onion *(finely chopped)*
1 large carrot *(finely chopped)*
2 garlic cloves *(minced)*
2 Tbsp extra virgin olive oil
3 ½ cups chicken broth
½ tsp ground nutmeg
salt and pepper to taste
¼ cup heavy cream *(optional)*

## Directions:

Brush cut side of squash with olive oil. Season with salt and pepper. Place cut side down on a baking pan. Bake at 400°F for 30 to 35 minutes or until squash is easily pricked with a fork.

In a 5 quart stock pot, sauté onion, carrot, and garlic in olive oil until tender. Season with salt and pepper.

Take squash that has been cooled to the touch, scoop out into the stock pot with onion mixture. Add the broth and simmer over medium heat for about 20 minutes or until squash is tender.

Use an immersion blender to puree the soup in the stock pot, or carefully put mixture into a blender no more than half full. Puree in batches and return to stock pot.

Stir in nutmeg and salt and pepper to taste.

If desired, add heavy cream (optional).

# Seaweed, Cabbage and Sausage Soup

*(Kaufmann 1)*

*by Melissa Henig*

*4 Servings*

## Ingredients:

1 Tbsp olive oil
1 yellow onion *(chopped)*
2 carrots *(chopped)*
2 celery stalks *(chopped)*
2 garlic cloves *(minced)*
2 grass-fed polish sausages
1 qt chicken broth
1 qt water
1 head cabbage *(chopped)*
1 cup Dulse Seaweed
2 Tbsp Italian seasoning
salt and pepper to taste

## Directions:

Heat a large skillet over medium heat. Add olive oil, onion, carrots, celery, and garlic. Sauté until golden brown.

In a separate pan cook the sausage. When done, cut into bite size rounds.

In large pot add broth and water. Add the sautéed vegetables, sausage, cabbage, seaweed, Italian seasoning, salt and pepper.

Cook on medium until the cabbage softens, about 20 minutes.

# Tomato Soup

*(Kaufmann 1)*

*6 to 8 Servings*

## Ingredients:

4 Tbsp *(½ stick)* butter
2 Tbsp extra virgin olive oil
1 medium onion *(finely chopped)*
salt and pepper to taste
3 Tbsp tomato paste
1 tsp dried thyme
2 cans (14 ½ oz) chicken broth
2 cans (28 oz) whole peeled tomatoes

fresh basil for garnish *(shredded)*

## Directions:

In a 5 quart Dutch oven, melt butter over medium heat; add oil and onion, season with salt and pepper. Cook until onion is translucent, about 5 minutes. Stir in tomato paste; cook 1 minute.

Add thyme, broth, and tomatoes. Bring to a boil; reduce heat and simmer 30 minutes. Break up tomatoes as it simmers.

Using an immersion blender, puree soup in the pot. You can also puree with a blender in batches. Only fill the blender about 1/3 of the way so hot soup doesn't expand and splash out all over you and the kitchen.

Make it as chunky or smooth as you like. Season with salt and pepper.

When serving, garnish with shredded basil.

# White Chicken Chili

*(Kaufmann 2)*

*This recipe serves 3 or 4 really hungry appetites. We recommend doubling the recipe which makes great leftovers.*

## Ingredients:

1 to 2 Tbsp extra virgin olive oil
1 onion *(diced)*
1 jalapeño (minced)
1 ½ lbs boneless, skinless chicken breasts *(cut into 1" pieces)*
3 garlic cloves *(minced)*
1 tsp chili powder
1 tsp ground cumin
¼ tsp cayenne pepper
1 ¼ tsp salt
2 cups chicken broth
2 (15 oz) cans white beans *(i.e. Cannellini – rinsed and drained) (mash about ½ cup or more with fork to help thicken the chili)*

## Directions:

In a large pot, heat olive oil over medium heat. Add onion and jalapeño and cook, stirring until the onion has softened, about 2 to 3 minutes.

Add the chicken and cook, stirring occasionally, until it is lightly browned on the outside and no longer pink on the inside (add more olive oil if needed), 5 to 10 minutes.

Add the minced garlic and spices and stir to coat the chicken. Let cook 1 minute.

Add a small amount of the chicken broth to deglaze the pan. Add the rest of the broth and stir in the beans and mashed beans. Bring to a boil. Reduce heat and simmer for about 20 minutes.

## CHAPTER 9

# Main Course

After you change your diet, many of the old staples you relied on for your big meals might be off limits now. However, when you begin eating on The Kaufmann Diet, you open yourself up to a wide variety of health-promoting foods. These main courses are delicious enough to be the center piece of a meal and nutritious enough to serve every day.

# Carne Asada (slow cooker)

*(Kaufmann 1)*

*4 to 6 Servings*

## Ingredients:

2 lbs skirt steak
salt and pepper
1 lime *(juiced)*
2 tsp cumin
1 tsp paprika
7 garlic cloves *(minced)*
2 tsp oregano
¼ cup fresh cilantro *(rough chopped)*

## Directions:

Cut skirt steak in half, thirds, or quarters so it will fit into your 6 quart slow cooker. Season with salt and pepper and set aside.

In a small bowl, mix together lime juice, cumin, paprika, garlic, and oregano.

Rub into the steak.

Place steak into a 6 quart slow cooker and sprinkle the cilantro on top.

Cook on low for 4 hours.

Remove the pot from the cooker, remove the lid and allow to rest for 10 to 15 minutes.

# Cauliflower Pizza Crust

*(Kaufmann 1)*

*by Joy Miller*

*Makes one 10" crust*

## Ingredients:

2 ½ Tbsp chia seeds
½ medium head of cauliflower
*(4 cups of small florets)*
⅓ cup almond flour
1 tsp dried oregano
¼ tsp garlic powder
½ tsp salt

## Directions:

Line a baking sheet with parchment paper, and set aside.

Mix chia seeds with ¼ water and refrigerate for 30 minutes.

Chop cauliflower into small florets, then steam until soft. Put into a colander and let drain until cool. Once cooled, put cauliflower into a clean dishtowel and squeeze out as much liquid as possible.

In a large bowl add the cauliflower and chia seed mixture and mash together with a fork.

Combine the almond flour, oregano, garlic powder and salt in a small bowl then add to the cauliflower mixture and mix well.

Form mixture into a ball and place on a parchment lined baking sheet. Pat down and work into about a 10" circle (about ¼" thick). You can also top with another piece of parchment to help press out while using a rolling pin.

Remove top layer of parchment and discard. Bake in a preheated 450°F oven for about 25 minutes or until lightly browned.

Add your favorite toppings and bake until everything is heated through, 8 to 10 minutes.

Allow to cool for a few minutes then enjoy.

# Chicken Picante

*(Kaufmann 2)*

*4 Servings*

## Ingredients:

4 boneless skinless chicken breasts
2 Tbsp extra virgin olive oil
2 cans black beans *(drained & rinsed)*
1 cup picante sauce *(chunky salsa)*

## Directions:

Preheat oven to 375°F.

Sear chicken with oil in a oven proof skillet, 2 to 3 minutes per side.

Mix the beans and picante sauce in a bowl and pour over chicken in skillet.

Bake 30 to 35 Minutes.

# Chicken Tikka Masala (slow cooker)

*(Kaufmann 1 or 2)*

*4 to 6 Servings*

## Ingredients:

2 lbs skinless, boneless chicken thighs *(cut into 1" cubes)*
salt and pepper
4 garlic cloves *(minced)*
2" piece ginger
*(peeled and finely grated)*
1 jalapeño pepper
*(seeded and finely diced)*
1 Tbsp paprika
2 tsp ground coriander
15 oz can crushed tomatoes
½ cup heavy cream *(optional)*
1 cup frozen peas
*(optional – Kaufmann 2)*
chopped fresh cilantro
*(for garnish)*

### Options:

Serve over these Kaufmann 1 or 2 friendly options: quinoa, brown rice or black rice.

## Directions:

Season the chicken with salt and pepper. Whisk the garlic, ginger, jalapeño, paprika, coriander, tomatoes, and ½ tsp salt in a 4 to 6 quart slow cooker. Add the chicken and stir to coat.

Cook on high for about 4 hours or low for about 6 hours. Add the heavy cream and frozen peas (if using) during the last 15 minutes of cooking.

Serve and garnish with cilantro.

# Chili Con Quinoa

*(Kaufmann 1)*

*by Jordan Palmer*

*6 to 8 servings*

This is a delicious Mexican style beef dish that can be eaten by itself or put on top of salads or soft tacos (Kaufmann 2).

## Ingredients:

2 Tbsp extra virgin olive oil
1 lb lean ground beef
2 large carrots *(diced)*
3 Tbsp chili powder
2 to 3 garlic cloves *(minced)*
1 tsp cumin
salt and pepper to taste
1 medium or large onion *(diced)*
1 bell pepper *(diced)*
2 to 3 cups cooked quinoa

Garnish:
lime zest & lime juice

## Directions:

In a large skillet on medium to medium high heat, add oil and coat the pan. Place ground beef, carrots, chili powder, garlic, cumin, salt, and pepper in the skillet and brown.

About half way through cooking the beef, add the onion and bell pepper.

Continue stirring and cooking until the beef is thoroughly cooked and the vegetables have reached their desired tenderness.

Stir in the quinoa and cook until heated through

Serve on your favorite mixed greens with a splash of lime juice to keep it Kaufmann 1 or serve on soft flour tortillas with lime zest for Kaufmann 2.

# Cuban Marinade

*(Kaufmann 1)*

This marinade is great on beef, chicken, or pork. Grill it, sauté it, or bake it anyway you like.

## Ingredients:

2 tsp garlic powder
1 tsp onion powder
1 tsp ground cumin
½ tsp dried oregano
½ tsp dried thyme
1 tsp dried cilantro
1 tsp dried parsley
1 tsp salt
½ tsp black pepper
4 Tbsp fresh lemon juice
3 Tbsp extra virgin olive oil

## Directions:

Mix all the ingredients together.

Put meat in an airtight container or large Ziploc bag. Pour marinade over the meat. Make sure all sides are covered with marinade. Put in the refrigerator and let sit for 2 to 3 hours.

# Grilled Mock Buttermilk Chicken

*(Kaufmann 1)*

*4 Servings*

## Ingredients:

3 lbs chicken *(cut up)* or your favorite chicken pieces
2 cups plain yogurt
½ cup water
2 tsp salt
1 tsp black or white pepper
¼ cup fresh thyme
8 garlic cloves *(smashed)*

## Directions:

Mix all ingredients (except chicken) together and pour over chicken in a dish and cover or put in gallon bag and marinate for 4 hours or overnight.

Heat grill to high.

Pat chicken dry and grill skin side down for 10 minutes over direct heat. Turn chicken over and continue to cook over indirect heat until done (20 to 25 minutes).

Let rest for 10 minutes and serve.

# Healthy Chili Tacos

*(Kaufmann 1 or 2)*

*by Melissa Henig*

*4 Servings*

## Ingredients:

1 bunch collard greens
I lb ground beef
2 tsp chili powder
1 tsp cumin
½ tsp salt
1 avocado *(sliced)*
1 tomato *(chopped)*
4 leaves romaine lettuce *(chopped)*
1 bunch cilantro *(chopped)*

### Garnish:

real sour cream *(Kaufmann 1)*
shredded Cheddar cheese *(Kaufmann 2)*

## Directions:

Steam the collards in a big pan of water on low for 15 to 20 minutes.

Sauté the ground beef in a large skillet, add chili powder, cumin and salt.

Place ground beef in steamed collard. Add avocado, tomato, lettuce and cilantro. Wrap up into a taco.

# Kaufmann Fettuccini Alfredo

## (aka: spaghetti squash with a cashew cream sauce)

*(Kaufman 1)*

*by Joy Miller*

*3 to 4 Servings*

### Ingredients:

1 medium size spaghetti squash
1 lb chicken breast
1 to 2 cups chopped broccoli
½ white onion *(minced)*
2 Tbsp avocado oil or ghee
salt and pepper to taste

**Cashew Cream Sauce:**

¾ cup raw cashews *(soaked in water 2 hours)*
½ cup coconut milk *(full fat or light)*
½ cup chicken broth

### Directions:

Preheat the oven to 375ºF.

Slice spaghetti squash in half lengthwise, and scoop out the seeds. Place the open sides down on a baking sheet. Bake for 40 to 45 minutes, or until tender enough to scrape out with a fork. Once done, use a fork to scrape out the squash in strands into a bowl.

While the squash bakes, cook the chicken. Season with salt and pepper then grill, bake, or sauté in a skillet until cooked through. Allow to rest for 5 minutes then cut or shred into bite sized pieces.

Blend the soaked cashews, coconut milk, and chicken broth in a blender until smooth. Set aside.

In a large skillet or pot over medium heat, sauté the broccoli, garlic, and onion in avocado oil or ghee until slightly softened (2 to 3 minutes). Add the sauce, and stir to combine. Continue to cook until the sauce is heated through (about 5 minutes).

Stir in the spaghetti squash and chicken. Season with salt and pepper and cook until heated through.

# Kheema: Indian Ground Meat

*(Kaufmann 1)*

*4 Servings*

## Ingredients:

3 Tbsp extra virgin olive oil
1 onion *(diced)*
4 garlic cloves *(minced)*
1" piece fresh ginger *(peeled and minced)*
2 tsp ground coriander
1 tsp paprika
½ tsp garam masala
½ tsp ground cumin
½ tsp cayenne pepper
1 lb ground meat *(beef, turkey, chicken)*
2 medium tomatoes *(chopped)*
salt and pepper to taste
2 tsp apple cider vinegar
¼ cup chopped cilantro *(more for garnish)*
Flat Bread for serving *(recipe in "Snacks & Appetizers" section)*

## Directions:

Heat olive oil in a large skillet or Dutch oven over medium-high heat. Add the onion and sauté until translucent, about 4 to 5 minutes. Add the garlic and ginger and cook for a another minute. Stir in the coriander, paprika, garam masala, cumin, and cayenne pepper. Cook for 1 minute.

Add the meat, break up with spoon and sauté until cooked through. Add tomatoes, 1 cup water and season with salt and pepper. Simmer for about 10 minutes.

Stir in the apple cider vinegar and cilantro.

Serve garnished with more cilantro and flat bread.

Great on its own or over quinoa.

# Meat Loaf

*(Kaufmann 1)*

*4 Servings*

## Ingredients:

1 lb ground beef or turkey
1 onion *(finely diced – raw or sautéed in olive oil)*
1 to 2 garlic cloves *(minced)*
1 cup quinoa flakes
½ cup tomato sauce *(more for top of loaf)*
¼ cup heavy cream
1 egg *(slightly beaten)*
1 tsp red pepper flakes *(or more to taste)*
¼ cup Italian parsley *(chopped)*
1 tsp dried thyme *(or more)*
salt and pepper to taste

## Directions:

Preheat oven to 350°F.

Put all the ingredients into a large mixing bowl and stir to combine. Using your hands is the easiest way. Make sure to wash you hands after handling raw meat.

Put the mixture onto a rimmed baking sheet or in a large baking dish and form into a loaf.

Spread about ¼ cup tomato sauce on top.

Bake for 45 minutes to an hour.

**Option:** Sauté a finely chopped carrot and red bell pepper with the onion for more flavor.

# Meatballs and Marinara Sauce

*(Kaufmann 1)*

*4 Servings*

## Ingredients:

**Sauce:**

2 Tbsp extra virgin olive oil
1 medium onion *(finely chopped, about ¾ cup)*
3 to 5 garlic cloves *(minced)*
3 Tbsp tomato paste
2 large cans (28 oz) crushed tomatoes
1 tsp dried oregano
1 tsp dried thyme
salt and pepper to taste

**Meatballs:**

1 lb lean ground meat *(beef, chicken or turkey)*
1 large egg *(slightly beaten)*
1 small onion *(finely chopped)*
½ cup Italian parsley *(chopped)*
¼ cup heavy whipping cream
½ cup quinoa flakes
1 tsp sea salt
¼ tsp pepper

## Directions:

**Make the sauce:**

Heat olive oil in large pot over medium to medium high heat. Sauté onion for 3 to 5 minutes until translucent. Add garlic and sauté 1 minute more. Add tomato paste, oregano, and thyme; stir and cook for another minute. Stir in crushed tomatoes, season with salt and pepper and simmer for 25 minutes.

**Make the meatballs:**

In a large bowl mix together ground meat, egg, onion, parsley, heavy cream, quinoa flakes, salt, and pepper. Mix with hands and form 12 uniform meatballs.

After the sauce has simmered for 25 minutes, drop the meatballs in the sauce (be careful), place in 1 layer, give them a little room. Cover with lid and let simmer for about 15 minutes until meatballs are cooked through.

Serve over steamed vegetables, spaghetti squash, or spiraled zucchini.

# Poached Salmon

*(Kaufmann 1)*

*by Lindsey Crouch*

*2 Servings*

## Ingredients:

2 wild caught salmon fillets *(skinless)*
¾ cup water
¾ cup chicken or vegetable broth
½ onion *(thinly sliced)*
1 garlic clove *(minced)*
salt and pepper to taste
fresh dill *(chopped)*

## Directions:

Add water and stock to a large skillet (50/50 Mixture), just enough to lay fish in without covering it.

Add onion and garlic and bring to a simmer.

Add salmon to skillet and season with salt and pepper.

Simmer about 5 to 7 minutes until desired doneness.

Remove from skillet and top with fresh dill.

# Quinoa Crusted Fish

*(Kaufmann 1)*

*4 Servings*

## Ingredients:

3 eggs
2 cups quinoa flakes
½ tsp ground cumin
1 or 2 tsp red pepper flakes
salt and pepper *(to taste)*
4 wild caught fish fillets
2 to 3 Tbsp extra virgin olive oil
cilantro, lime wedges and lime zest for garnish

## Directions:

Place the eggs in a bowl and whisk with a fork.

Place the quinoa flakes, cumin, red pepper flakes, salt, and pepper in a bowl and mix together.

Dip the fish into the egg and press into the quinoa mixture to coat.

Heat about 2 Tbsp extra virgin olive oil in a large frying pan over medium heat.

Cook the fish about 3 minutes on each side until golden and cooked through.

Garnish with cilantro, lime wedges and lime zest.

# Roast Chicken with Lemon & Garlic

*(Kaufmann 1)*

*4 Servings*

## Ingredients:

3 to 4 lb whole chicken *(patted dry)*
salt and pepper to taste
1 head garlic *(halved crosswise)*
1 lemon *(halved and seeds removed)*
½ stick butter *(melted)*

## Directions:

Preheat oven to 425°F with rack in middle position.

With chicken breast facing up and legs toward you, use a sharp knife to slice through loose area of skin between leg and breast. This helps for a more even cooking for the thickest part of the chicken.

Season the chicken inside and out with salt and pepper.

Lay the chicken, breast side up, in a large oven proof skillet. Place the garlic and lemon, cut sides down, around the chicken then drizzle the butter over the chicken.

Cook until browned and cooked through for about 45 minutes. An instant read thermometer should read 160° in the thickest part of the thigh or until the juices run clear when poked with a knife.

Let the chicken rest for at least 10 minutes in the skillet before carving.

Serve topped with pan juices and with roasted lemon and garlic.

# Sausage and Broccoli Frittata

*(Kaufmann 1)*

*8 Servings*

## Ingredients:

12 large eggs
½ cup unsweetened coconut milk
salt and pepper to taste
2 Tbsp extra virgin olive oil
½ onion *(diced)*
½ lb chorizo *(any favorite sausage, casings removed)*
1 head broccoli *(florets cut into bitesize)*

Garnishes: sliced tomatoes, basil, parsley

## Directions:

Preheat broiler.

Whisk eggs and milk in a medium bowl. Season with salt and pepper then set aside.

Heat oil in a large oven proof skillet (cast iron works best) over medium heat. Add onion and chorizo (or sausage) and cook until onion is softened and chorizo is crumbled and brown, 6 to 8 minutes.

Add broccoli and season with salt and pepper. Cook stirring occasionally until broccoli is tender or desired doneness, about 8 to 10 minutes.

Reduce heat to low and pour whisked eggs into the skillet covering everything. Cook, shaking pan from time to time until edges are set, about 10 to 12 minutes.

Put skillet in oven and broil until the top is golden brown and center is set. Make sure you stay near the oven and keep and eye on your frittata so it doesn't burn.

Remove from oven and let set for a couple of minutes before slicing into wedges.

# Slow Cooker Pot Roast

*(Kaufmann 1)*

*4 to 6 Servings*

## Ingredients:

4 lb beef chuck roast
1 medium yellow onion *(rough chop)*
2 medium sweet potatoes *(peeled and cubed)*
2 medium carrots *(cut 1" pieces)*
2 medium parsnips *(cut 1" pieces)*
2 stalks celery *(cut 1" pieces)*
2 to 4 garlic cloves *(minced)*
1 ½ cups beef broth
2 tsp dried thyme
salt and pepper to taste

## Directions:

Season roast with salt and pepper and lay inside the center of a 6 quart slow cooker. If you have time, you can also sear your roast in a skillet with a little olive oil before adding it to the slow cooker.

Arrange onion, sweet potatoes, carrots, parsnips, and celery around roast. Sprinkle garlic over everything.

Pour in beef broth then season with thyme and more salt and pepper.

Cover and cook on low for about 7 to 8 hours.

# Spicy Coconut Chicken

*(Kaufmann 1)*

*4 Servings*

## Ingredients:

1 Tbsp extra virgin olive oil
4 whole chicken legs
*(with thighs, about 3 lbs)*
coarse salt and ground pepper
1 can (14.5 oz) light coconut milk
1 ½ cups chicken broth
½ cup water
2 Tbsp red curry paste
*(check the ingredients)*
1 cup quinoa *(rinsed)*
2 red bell peppers
*(seeded and cut into 1" pieces)*
2 medium zucchini
*(cut into half moon slices)*

## Directions:

In a large Dutch oven or heavy pot, heat oil over medium high. Season chicken with salt and pepper. Cook chicken in batches until browned, 6 to 8 minutes. Transfer to a plate for further cooking later.

Add coconut milk, broth, ½ cup water, and curry paste to the pot and bring to a boil. Stir in quinoa. Nestle chicken (with juices) in pot, cover and reduce heat to medium low. Cook without stirring for about 15 minutes.

Sprinkle bell peppers and zucchini on top of chicken mixture and cover.

Cook until vegetables are crisp tender, about 8 to 10 minutes.

**Tip:** For a little more flavor, sauté zucchini in a tablespoon of olive oil until slightly browned before adding to pot.

# Spicy Indian Butter Chicken (slow cooker)

*(Kaufmann 1)*

*4 Servings*

## Ingredients:

1 cup plain yogurt
1 Tbsp lemon juice
2 tsp ground cumin
1 tsp ground cinnamon
1 tsp cayenne pepper
¾ tsp black pepper
1 tsp ground ginger
1 tsp salt
3 to 4 boneless skinless chicken breasts *(cut into 1" cubes)*

## Sauce:

1 Tbsp butter
1 clove garlic *(minced)*
1 jalapeño pepper *(finely chopped)*
2 tsp ground cumin
2 tsp paprika
1 tsp salt
8 oz can tomato sauce
1 cup coconut milk *(full fat)*
2 Tbsp tapioca flour
1 Tbsp water

## Directions:

In a large resealable bag (the night before cooking) add the yogurt, lemon juice, cumin, cinnamon, cayenne, black pepper, ginger, salt, and chicken. Seal the bag and work the mixture into the chicken until all incorporated. Let sit in the refrigerator overnight.

When you're ready to cook the chicken, put the butter, garlic, and jalapeño into the bottom of the slow cooker. Remove the chicken from the marinade, scraping off the majority of it and put the chicken into the slow cooker. Discard remaining marinade.

In a small bowl combine the cumin, paprika, salt, tomato sauce, and heavy cream and stir. Pour the sauce over the chicken, cover and cook on low for 4 to 5 hours.

Mix the tapioca flour with the water then add to the slow cooker and stir. Cook an additional 20 minutes on high.

Serve over quinoa and garnish with cilantro.

# Steak Rolls

*(Kaufmann 1)*

*by Joy Miller*

*8 Servings*

## Ingredients:

8 thin slices of sirloin or flank steak
*(about 4 or 5" wide x 8" long)*
extra virgin olive oil
salt and pepper to taste
fresh rosemary *(chopped)*
1 red bell pepper
*(sliced into thin strips)*
1 yellow bell pepper
*(sliced into thin strips)*
1 medium zucchini
*(sliced into thin strips)*
1 medium yellow onion
*(halved and thinly sliced)*

## Directions:

If the meat is a little thick use a mallet to flatten it a little.

Rub each side of the steak slices with a little oil. Sprinkle with salt, fresh ground black pepper and chopped rosemary. (You can also make your favorite marinade and let the meat sit in that for an hour or so.)

Heat a tablespoon of olive oil in a skillet over medium high heat and cook the vegetables until crisp-tender, season with salt and pepper. Transfer to a plate.

Place some of the vegetable strips vertically on one end of each steak cutlet so when rolled up the end of the vegetables are sticking out of each end of the steak roll.

Roll it up, and secure it with a toothpick. Repeat for each steak roll.

Cook on a grill, on each side for about 2 to 3 minutes (or to desired doneness) or cook them in a skillet on medium to medium high heat until done.

# Sweet Garlic Butter Glazed Salmon

*(Kaufmann 2)*

*2 Servings*

## Ingredients:

3 Tbsp unsalted butter
1 garlic clove *(minced)*
1 Tbsp honey
2 Tbsp lemon juice
2 tsp extra virgin olive oil
2 (6 oz) salmon fillets

## Directions:

Combine butter, garlic, and honey in a small sauce pan.

Simmer for about a minute or until it turns golden.

Add lemon juice and swirl pan to mix. Set aside.

Heat olive oil in a non-stick skillet over moderately high heat until hot and cook salmon 2 to 3 minutes per side until just cooked through.

Put salmon on serving plates and drizzle over salmon fillets and serve.

# Tex-Mex Spaghetti Squash

*(Kaufmann 2)*

*2 Large Servings*

## Ingredients:

1 medium spaghetti squash
1 Tbsp extra virgin olive oil
sea salt & pepper to taste
3 to 4 oz cooked chicken breast *(cut into chunks)*
1 cup black beans *(rinsed & drained)*
1 cup salsa
3 Tbsp cilantro *(chopped)*
1 to 2 tsp red pepper flakes *(optional)*

## Directions:

Preheat oven to 425°F and line a baking sheet with parchment paper.

Cut the squash in half and remove the seeds. Rub the inside with olive oil and season with salt and pepper. Place the 2 halves face down on a baking sheet and bake for 25 to 30 minutes. The edges on the inside should be a bit browned and shred easily with a fork. If not, bake a few minutes more.

Let the squash cool for about 5 minutes and set the oven to broil.

Shred the squash into a large bowl (be careful while handling the hot squash, use a towel to hold). Add the chicken, beans, salsa and cilantro and mix to combine.

Split the mixture in half and stuff each squash shell. Sprinkle with red pepper flakes.

Place them back on the same baking sheet & broil for about 3 to 4 minutes.

Garnish with avocado slices and lime wedges.

# Thai Turkey Meatballs

*(Kaufmann 1)*

*by Abby Miller*

*4 Servings*

This recipe has several ingredients which when purchasing, make sure you check the ingredients on the labels to see if they are Kaufmann 1 friendly.

## Ingredients:

**Meatballs:**

2 lbs ground turkey
2 eggs *(slightly beaten)*
2 tsp grated ginger
2 garlic cloves *(minced)*
2 Tbsp chopped basil
¼ cup chopped green onions
1 cup finely chopped cabbage
2 Tbsp light coconut milk
1 tsp red curry paste *(check the ingredients)*
1 Tbsp fish sauce
⅛ tsp red pepper flakes *(more to taste)*
1 tsp salt

**Sauce:**

1½ cup light coconut milk
3 Tbsp tomato paste
1 tsp red curry paste
1 tsp fish sauce
⅛ tsp red pepper flakes *(more to taste)*

2 to 4 Tbsp olive oil *(for cooking)*

## Directions:

In a large bowl, combine meatball ingredients and mix with your hands thoroughly. Make meatballs any size you like and set aside on a platter.

In a small bowl, whisk the sauce ingredients together and set aside.

Preheat a large skillet on medium high heat and add some olive oil and swirl in pan. Add meatballs and cook until brown and almost cooked through, turning a few times. Add the sauce, reduce heat to medium and simmer for 15 to 20 minutes, uncovered.

Serve warm over quinoa or by themselves.

# Tuna Casserole

*(Kaufmann 2)*

*by Melissa Henig*

*4 Servings*

## Ingredients:

1 head cauliflower *(chopped into small pieces)*
4 Tbsp olive or coconut oil *(divided)*
2 garlic cloves *(minced)*
2 Tbsp dried thyme
1 Tbsp dried sage
5 Tbsp almond flour
½ tsp salt
½ tsp black pepper
1 can coconut milk *(full fat)*
2 cans tuna fish
1 cup green peas

**Garnish:**

¼ tsp nutmeg
chopped fresh parsley

## Directions:

Preheat the oven to 375°F. Grease a 9x13" pan with 1 Tbsp of oil.

Put cauliflower in a pan, cover with water and bring to a boil over high heat. Reduce heat and let simmer for about 5 minutes or until tender. Drain.

In a large skillet over medium heat add 3 Tbsp of oil.

Add garlic, thyme, sage, almond flour, salt and pepper. Slowly stir in the coconut milk and whisk with the flour removing all the lumps as you go along.

Stir in the tuna and heat through letting the sauce thicken.

Place the cauliflower in the prepared pan and pour the sauce over the top. Sprinkle the peas over the dish.

Cover and bake for 15 minutes. Uncover and bake for another 10 minutes to slightly brown.

Garnish with nutmeg and parsley.

# Vegetarian Stuffed Peppers (slow cooker)

*(Kaufmann 2)*

*4 to 6 Servings*

## Ingredients:

5 to 6 large bell peppers *(any color)*
1 can (15 oz) cannellini beans *(rinsed and drained)*
½ cup crumbled goat cheese
1 cup cooked quinoa
4 scallions *(sliced)*
2 garlic cloves *(minced)*
1 tsp dried oregano
salt and pepper to taste

## Directions:

Slice a thin layer from the base of the pepper so they stand flat. Slice off the tops just below the stem and discard the stem and chop the tops and place in a mixing bowl. Remove the seeds and ribs from the inside of the peppers.

In mixing bowl, add beans, goat cheese, quinoa, scallions, garlic, and oregano. Season with salt and pepper. Mix to combine with a fork. Mash some of the beans with fork while mixing.

Place peppers standing up in the slow cooker, cover and cook on high for 2.5 to 3 hours.

# Yogurt Parmesan Chicken

*(Kaufmann 2)*

*4 Servings*

## Ingredients:

4 boneless/skinless chicken breast *(patted dry)*
olive oil *(for baking sheet)*
1 cup plain Greek yogurt
½ cup grated Parmesan cheese
1 tsp garlic powder
salt and pepper to taste

## Directions:

Preheat oven to 375°F. Lightly oil a rimmed baking sheet with olive oil.

Combine yogurt, Parmesan cheese, garlic powder, salt and pepper in a medium to large bowl.

Add the chicken breasts and coat well. Let sit for about 15 minutes.

Place chicken on baking sheet and bake for about 45 minutes. Remove from oven and let rest for at least 5 minutes before serving.

## CHAPTER 10

# Side Dishes

No main course is complete without a variety of delicious sides. Skip the potatoes, pasta, and other sides; here you will find some fresh, healthy, and Kaufmann Diet-approved recipes to round out your dinner table.

# Broccoli with Tomatoes

*(Kaufmann 2)*

## Ingredients:

1 lb fresh broccoli
*(trim and use florets)*
2 Tbsp extra virgin olive oil
2 garlic cloves *(minced)*
2 small tomatoes *(chopped)*
¼ cup sun dried tomatoes *(chopped)*
¼ cup water
½ tsp salt *(or to taste)*
2 to 3 Tbsp crumbled goat cheese
2 Tbsp pine nuts

## Directions:

Heat olive oil in large sauté pan over medium high heat.

Add broccoli and stir-fry for about 2 to 3 minutes, until just beginning to soften.

Add garlic, fresh tomatoes, sun dried tomatoes, and ¼ cup water. Continue to stir until sauce in pan just begins to thicken, about 3 minutes more.

Reduce heat to medium and cover pan. Cook for about 2 to 5 minutes, checking for doneness. (Broccoli should be crisp tender.) Season with sea salt.

Pour into serving bowl and top with goat cheese and pine nuts.

# Cauliflower Stuffing

*(Kaufmann 1)*

*4 to 6 Servings*

## Ingredients:

4 Tbsp unsalted butter
1 onion *(diced)*
2 large carrots *(peeled and diced)*
2 celery stalks *(diced)*
1 small head cauliflower *(chopped)*
salt and pepper to taste
½ tsp poultry seasoning *(optional)*
¼ cup chopped fresh parsley
2 Tbsp chopped fresh rosemary
1 Tbsp chopped fresh sage
½ cup vegetable or chicken broth

## Directions:

In a large skillet over medium heat, melt butter then add onion, carrot, and celery. Sauté until soft, about 7 to 8 minutes.

Add cauliflower and season with salt, pepper, and poultry seasoning. Cook until tender for another 8 to 10 minutes.

Stir in the parsley, rosemary, and sage then add the broth and simmer slightly covered until the liquid is absorbed and flavors have combined, about 10 to 15 minutes. If there is any remaining liquid remove lid to let it cook down.

# Garlic Roasted Sweet Potatoes & Onions

*(Kaufmann 2)*

*by Lindsey Crouch*

*6 Servings*

## Ingredients:

4 medium sweet potatoes *(peeled and cut into 2" chunks) (about 2 ¼ pounds)*
2 medium sweet onions *(rough cut)*
4 garlic cloves *(minced)*
2 Tbsp extra virgin olive oil
salt and pepper to taste

## Directions:

Preheat oven to 425°F.

Toss potatoes, onions, and garlic on a large roasting pan. Drizzle with olive oil and season with salt and pepper. Toss to coat all the vegetables.

Bake for 30 to 35 minutes, stirring occasionally, until potatoes are tender.

# Italian Style Quinoa

*(Kaufmann 1)*

*by Melissa Henig*

*2 Servings*

## Ingredients:

1 cup uncooked quinoa *(rinsed and drained)*
1 cup chopped cherry tomatoes
1 handful of basil *(torn or shredded)*
4 Tbsp extra virgin olive oil
3 Tbsp butter
salt and pepper to taste

## Directions:

Cook the quinoa in a medium saucepan with 2 cups of water. Bring to a boil in a over high heat. Reduce heat to low, cover and simmer until tender and most of the liquid has been absorbed, 15 to 20 minutes.

Stir in the tomatoes, basil, olive oil, butter, salt and pepper then serve.

# Lemon-Almond Broccoli

*(Kaufmann 1)*

*2 to 4 Servings*

## Ingredients:

1 large head broccoli *(cut into florets)*
4 Tbsp butter *(melted)*
2 Tbsp lemon juice
¼ cup blanched almonds

## Directions:

Steam or boil broccoli until desired tenderness.

In the meantime, melt the butter in a saucepan over medium heat. Remove from heat and add the lemon juice and almonds.

Drain broccoli and put into a serving dish, pour the butter mixture over the broccoli and serve.

# Mashed Cauliflower

*(Kaufmann 1)*

*4 Servings*

## Ingredients:

1 head cauliflower *(cut into florets)*

2 garlic cloves *(more or less)*

1 Tbsp extra virgin olive oil

salt and pepper to taste

## Directions:

Place a steamer insert into a pot or saucepan and fill with water to just below the bottom of the steamer. Bring water to a boil. Add cauliflower and garlic then cover and steam until tender, about 10 minutes. Note: You can also boil the cauliflower and garlic if you don't have a steamer.

Add cauliflower, garlic, and olive oil to a food processor and process until smooth. Add more oil for desired consistency. Season with salt and pepper.

Get creative and add different spices or throw some scallions or chives in during processing.

# Roasted Acorn Squash

*(Kaufmann 1)*

*4 Servings*

## Ingredients:

2 medium acorn squash *(halved and seeded)*

1 to 2 Tbsp extra virgin olive oil

Coarse salt and cracked pepper to taste

## Directions:

Preheat oven to 400°F.

Brush cut side of squash with olive oil. Season with salt and pepper.

Place cut side down on a baking pan.

Bake for 30 to 35 minutes or until squash is easily pricked with a fork.

# Roasted Cauliflower

*(Kaufmann 1)*

*4 to 6 Servings*

## Ingredients:

1 head cauliflower
1 ½ cups plain Greek yogurt
1 lime *(zest and juice)*
2 Tbsp chili powder
1 Tbsp cumin
1 Tbsp garlic powder
1 tsp curry powder
2 tsp salt
1 tsp black pepper

## Directions:

Preheat oven to 400°F.

Lightly grease a baking sheet.

Trim the base of the cauliflower so it lays flat. Make sure to remove any green leaves and stems.

In a bowl combine all other ingredients: yogurt, lime zest, lime juice, chili powder, cumin, garlic powder, curry powder, salt, and pepper.

Dip the cauliflower into the mixture and roll around to cover the entire top. Place it on the baking sheet and spread more of the mixture to make a thick coating all over the top and sides. (Save any extra yogurt mixture for other uses.)

Bake for about 40 minutes. Check by piercing with a skewer or pointed knife until desired tenderness.

Let cool for about 5 minutes. Slice and serve.

# Sautéed Chickpeas

*(Kaufmann 2)*

*4 Servings*

## Ingredients:

2 (15.5 oz) cans chickpeas
*(rinsed, drained, patted dry)*
4 garlic cloves (minced)
⅓ cup extra virgin olive oil
salt and pepper to taste
¾ cup chopped parsley
¾ cup chopped chives
¾ cup chopped basil

## Directions:

Heat oil in a large skillet or Dutch oven over medium heat.

Add the chickpeas and cook, stirring occasionally, until golden brown, 10 to 15 minutes. Season with salt and pepper.

Remove from heat, put in a bowl and stir in herbs.

You can use any herbs you like. Mix it up and make it different with cilantro.

# Sautéed Kale

*(Kaufmann 1)*

*by Abby Miller*

*2 Servings*

## Ingredients:

1 Tbsp butter
1 bunch fresh kale
*(chopped and stems removed)*
½ red onion *(diced)*
1 clove garlic *(minced)*
3 slices bacon
*(cooked and chopped)*
salt and pepper to taste

## Directions:

Heat a large skillet to about medium heat and melt butter.

Add onion and sauté until translucent, about 3 to 4 minutes. Add garlic and cook 30 seconds more.

Add kale to pan, sauté and toss with tongs until it's about half it's original size.

Add bacon and season with salt and pepper. Serve warm.

# Spinach with Shallots

*(Kaufmann 1)*

*by Joy Miller*

*2 Servings*

## Ingredients:

1 Tbsp extra virgin olive oil
1 large shallot *(diced)*
10 oz or more baby spinach
salt and pepper to taste
juice of ½ lemon

## Directions:

In a large skillet, heat olive oil over medium heat. Stir in shallots and cook until transparent, about 4 to 5 minutes.

Add spinach, sprinkle with salt and pepper; cook and stir for 3 to 5 minutes until leaves are wilted and reduced.

Serve warm with a splash of fresh lemon juice.

# CHAPTER 11

# Desserts

Dessert must be off limits if you are on a diet, right? Think again. Here you will find a variety of Kaufmann Diet-approved desserts that are sure to satisfy your sweet tooth without wrecking your diet, or your health. Find out here how dessert can be both satisfying and healthy.

# Blueberry Almond Bread

*(Kaufmann 1)*

*by Jordan Palmer*

*8 to 10 Servings*

## Ingredients:

butter for pan
1 ½ cups almond flour
½ cup arrowroot flour
1 tsp baking soda
½ tsp salt
3 large eggs
½ tsp vanilla extract
10 to 15 drops of liquid stevia *(or desired sweetness)*
1 Tbsp apple cider vinegar
2 Tbsp avocado oil *(or other Kaufmann friendly oil)*
⅓ cup blueberries
sliced almonds *(for topping)*

## Directions:

Preheat oven to 350°F with a rack in the middle position. Butter a 9x5" loaf pan and set aside.

In a large bowl, mix the dry ingredients; almond flour, arrowroot flour, baking soda and salt. Set aside.

In another bowl add the eggs and beat with a whisk. Add the stevia, vinegar, and oil then whisk together.

Add the wet ingredients to the dry ingredients and mix until combined well.

Carefully stir in the blueberries and let the batter rest for about 5 minutes.

Pour the batter into the prepared loaf pan and top with sliced almonds.

Bake for 30 to 35 minutes. Test with a toothpick.

**Note:** This recipe also works well with sliced strawberries. Just substitute ⅓ cup sliced strawberries for the blueberries.

# Cheesecake with Nutmeal Pie Crust

*(Kaufmann 1)*

*8 Servings*

## Ingredients:

### Crust:

2 cups walnuts *(or other Kaufmann friendly nuts)*

3 Tbsp butter (melted)

### Filling:

16 oz cream cheese *(softened)*

⅓ to ½ cup xylitol *(or stevia to taste)*

2 large eggs

1 tsp vanilla extract

1 tsp lemon zest *(optional)*

## Directions:

For The Crust: Preheat oven to 350°F. Put nuts into a food processor and process until fine. Combine with the butter and press into a 9" pie pan and bake for 12 minutes. Remove from oven and let cool.

For The Filling: Lower oven to 325°F. In a large mixing bowl, using an electric mixer, combine the cream cheese and sweetener. Beat until smooth. Add the eggs one at a time then add the vanilla and lemon zest.

Place the prepared pie shell on a baking sheet and pour the cream cheese mixture into the pie shell.

Bake for about 25 minutes or until the center is almost set. The center should move when jiggled.

Let cool and refrigerate for 2 to 3 hours.

Slice and top with your favorite Kaufmann friendly berries.

# Chocolate Avocado Pudding

*(Kaufmann 2)*

*(by Joy Miller)*

*4 Servings*

## Ingredients:

3 avocados
6 Tbsp cocoa
*(or cacao)* powder
¼ cup honey
1 tsp pure vanilla extract

## Directions:

Put all the ingredients in a food processor and process until smooth.

Adjust the sweetness to your liking.

# Chocolate Brownies

*(Kaufmann 2)*

*by Jordan Palmer*

*9 Servings*

## Ingredients:

1½ cups almond flour
¾ cup arrowroot flour
¼ cup flax seed meal
½ tsp baking soda
2 Tbsp cocoa powder
¼ tsp salt
3 large eggs
⅓ cup maple syrup *(or honey)*
1 tsp apple cider vinegar
½ tsp liquid stevia *(chocolate flavored liquid stevia optional)*
¼ cup chopped walnuts *(optional)*

## Directions:

Preheat oven to 350°F.

Prepare a 8x8" baking pan by greasing it with butter.

Mix the dry ingredients in a large mixing bowl. Beat the eggs, vinegar, and stevia in another bowl.

Pour the wet ingredients in with the dry ingredients and stir together until combined.

Bake for 20 to 25 minutes. Insert toothpick in center to see if it comes out clean.

# Chocolate Cream Pie

*(Kaufmann 1)*

*by Joy Miller*

*6 Servings*

## Ingredients:

**Pie Crust:**

1½ cup almond meal flour

2 Tbsp butter *(room temperature)*

Mix with a fork and press into a 9" pie plate. Bake at 350°F for about 10 minutes. Let completely cool.

**Chocolate Filling:**

2 large ripe avocados

2 Tbsp butter *(room temperature)*

½ cup cocoa powder

liquid stevia *(to taste)*

1 cup heavy cream

1 tsp pure vanilla extract

## Directions:

Put avocados, butter, and cocoa powder in a food processor and process until smooth. Scrape down sides of processor bowl and pulse a few more times.

Add desired amount of liquid stevia and process, checking for sweetness.

**Note:** you can use about 3 Tbsp honey as a substitute for stevia, but that will make the recipe Kaufmann 2.

In a separate bowl, whip heavy cream, vanilla, and 4 to 5 drops of liquid stevia until hard peaks form. Fold into chocolate mixture then spread into the cooled pie shell.

Refrigerate until firm and ready to serve.

# Fried Apples

*(Kaufmann 1)*

*by Abby Miller*

*4 Servings*

## Ingredients:

4 to 5 green apples
ground cinnamon *(to taste)*
stevia or xylitol *(to taste)*
1 to 2 Tbsp coconut oil

## Directions:

Core apples and cut into slices. The thicker the slice, the longer it will take to cook.

Heat a skillet to medium heat and add the coconut oil. When the oil is melted and the pan is coated with the oil, toss in the apples and cook for 5 to 10 minutes, stirring often. You want the apples to be softer, but not mushy.

Add desired amount of cinnamon and sweetener, stirring until the apples are thoroughly coated.

Remove from heat and serve.

Can be used as a side dish instead of sugar free apple sauce, added to yogurt for breakfast, or as a dessert with a toasted nuts and whipped cream on top.

# Frozen Lime Bars

*(Kaufmann 2)*

*by Abby Miller*

*9 Servings*

## Ingredients:

### Crust:

1 ½ cup almond flour
4 Tbsp butter *(melted)*
stevia to taste

### Pie Filling:

1 ½ cups raw cashews
1 cup full-fat coconut milk
⅔ cup fresh lime juice *(about 5 to 7 large limes)*
½ cup honey
⅓ cup coconut oil *(melted)*
1 Tbsp lime zest

## Directions:

Soak the cashews: Place the cashews in a bowl and cover with water. Let sit at room temperature for 2 to 6 hours or in the refrigerator overnight. Drain before using.

For the crust: combine almond flour, butter, and stevia in a bowl and mix to combine. Press into a 8x8" baking pan.

Bake crust for about 10 minutes at 350°F. Let cool completely.

For the filling: Place all the ingredients except the lime zest into a high-speed blender. Blend until smooth. Add the lime zest and pulse to combine. Pour the mixture on top of the crust. Place the pan in the freezer for 2 to 4 hours until set.

Slice and serve frozen.

Bars will keep in the freezer for up to a week.

# Lemon Walnut Bread

*(Kaufmann 1)*

*by Jordan Palmer*

*Makes one 9" round*

## Ingredients:

2¼ cups almond flour
1 cup xylitol
*(or other granulated sweetener)*
1 tsp baking soda
¼ tsp salt
4 large eggs
1 Tbsp apple cider vinegar
1 tsp vanilla extract
3 Tbsp avocado oil
zest and juice of 2 small lemons
½ cup walnuts *(small pieces)*

## Directions:

Preheat the oven to 350°F.

In a large bowl, add the almond flour, sweetener, baking soda, and salt. Sift together with a wire whisk. Set aside.

In a food processor add the eggs, apple cider vinegar, vanilla, and avocado oil. Blend on high for 1 minute.

Add the wet ingredients to the dry ingredients and stir to combine. Stir in the lemon zest and walnuts.

Spoon the mixture into a round greased 9" cake pan and bake for 30 to 35 minutes. Test with a toothpick for doneness.

*We used a cake pan and sliced into wedges. You could use a loaf pan and experiment with the cooking times.

# Pumpkin Parfait

*(Kaufmann 2)*

*by Joy Miller*

*2 Servings*

## Ingredients:

**Pudding:**

1 cup pumpkin
1 cup almond milk
1 tsp cinnamon
*(or pumpkin pie spice)*
1 tsp vanilla
2 Tbsp honey *(or maple syrup)*
5 Tbsp chia seeds

**Whipped Topping:**

1 can of coconut milk
4 drops of stevia
*(or honey to taste)*

**Garnish:**

Cinnamon to sprinkle on top
Cinnamon stick for decoration

## Directions:

Combine first 5 ingredients (pumpkin, almond milk, cinnamon, vanilla, honey) in blender. Put in a storage container and mix in the chia seeds, cover and put in refrigerator for several hours or overnight. The chia seeds will expand and thicken the mixture.

**Whipped Topping:**

Place the can of coconut milk in the freezer for several hours or in the refrigerator overnight.

When ready, scoop out the thicker cream that has formed on top and put into a mixing bowl. Reserve the remaining liquid for another use. Whip the coconut cream until it reaches a whipped cream consistency. Add sweetener to taste. Cover and put in refrigerator to thicken more.

To make the parfait, spoon alternating layers of pudding and whipped topping into a parfait or drinking glass, ending with the whipped topping on top. Sprinkle cinnamon on top. You can place a cinnamon stick in the side for decoration.

# Recipe Index

## N



## O



## P



## Q



## S

# The Kaufmann Diets

Fungi are known human parasites. They can enter our body in many ways, from inhalation, to foods contaminated with fungus that wind up in our food supply, which is not uncommon. Several of the fungal species in our air and food supply make poisonous substances called mycotoxins.

The study of fungal poisons is a relatively new field of science. Its genesis occurred in England in the early 1960s when thousands of turkeys died from eating peanut meal that was impregnated with mycotoxins. We know that fungal mycotoxins can cause illness and death in animals and humans. In the 1970s, when I began studying fungal diseases, I realized that peanuts were not the only foods that were contaminated with mycotoxins. From the scant literature on mycotoxins that existed in the 1970s, I developed a diet that minimized exposure to these known fungal poisons. Today, we know significantly more about foods that starve fungal parasites, and those foods are updated and included in The Kaufmann 1 and Kaufmann 2 Diets.

The premises for avoiding foods that feed fungi are quite simple. Avoid yeast foods like baker's yeast and brewer's yeast. Avoid foods that are contaminated with fungal mycotoxins, like grains and alcoholic beverages. Avoid eating fungi, itself, in the form of mushrooms, myco-protein and other foods. Avoid eating foods high in sugar and carbohydrates, which fungi and yeasts need to survive. These premises have remained the same for decades in my books and diets.

Advancements in my understanding of how fungus actually causes us to crave the foods required for its own survival (sugars/carbohydrates), and of foods that are either contaminated with or feed fungus, continue to this day. This 2018 update represents updated information on my understandings of these advancements. Additionally, the diets consider food allergies and food addictions that many people have, because the most common allergic offenders are avoided on The Kaufmann Diets.

If you are sick, always work with a healthcare professional when initiating dietary changes. If the underlying reason you are sick is linked to fungus, The Kaufmann Diets, although perhaps initially causing a "die-off" reaction in some people for a short time, may have you feeling significant improvement within a few weeks.

# The Kaufmann 1 Diet

## 1. Sugar/Sweeteners

**Allowed:** Stevia is allowed, along with xylitol made from corncob or birch tree bark

**Excluded:** No added sugar is allowed while following the Kaufmann 1 Diet, including honey, agave, or other "natural" sweeteners. Aspartame and other artificial sweeteners are not allowed on the diet.

## 2. Fruit

**Allowed:** Green apples, berries, avocados, fresh coconut, grapefruit, lemons, limes, and tomatoes

**Excluded:** Virtually all other fruits are excluded from the Kaufmann 1 Diet, usually due to the higher fructose content.

## 3. Meat

**Allowed:** Virtually all fresh, minimally processed meats. These include, beef, lamb, bison, turkey, chicken, pork, venison, etc. This also includes fish such as salmon, tuna, and shellfish. Wild-caught fish and grass-fed or pasture-raised meats are always preferable. Avoid conventionally raised meat and farmed fish, whenever possible, as added antibiotics and/or hormones may affect fungal proliferation.

**Excluded:** Beware of meats that have been cured using sugar, processed meats or deli meats which often contain sugar and/or ingredients such as wheat, corn, etc. Avoid breaded meats, as well.

## 4. Eggs

**Allowed:** All eggs are allowed, but pastured eggs are best, because the chickens that laid the eggs have a more natural diet and environment.

**Excluded:** Egg substitutes.

## 5. Dairy

Keep in mind that dairy foods are often allergy foods. Dairy products can also be mucous-producing. As a general rule, the dairy foods chosen on the Kaufmann 1 Diet are high in fat and low in milk sugar (lactose). As you consider using dairy products while on the Kaufmann 1 Diet, consider also that dairy products can be addicting, and the diets are meant to assist you in breaking those addictions. Do you eat dairy products daily? Most of us do. If you are not allergic to dairy foods, and you are not over consuming them currently, you can enjoy them minimally while on the Kaufmann 1 Diet.

**Allowed:**

**BUTTER** is a high fat product, but as such, contains only tiny amounts of lactose.

**GHEE** is clarified butter.

**YOGURT** Goat yogurt, in moderation, is OK. Live cultured dairy probiotics contain relatively little lactose. Try to get higher-fat yogurt with live bacterial cultures.

**HEAVY CREAM** is the fat skimmed off the top of milk, which creates heavy cream, and it is about 37% fat. It contains almost no lactose (sugar), making it favorable on this diet. Therefore, **unsweetened whipping cream**, since it is heavy cream, is also OK.

**SOUR CREAM** Look for varieties made from real cream. There are now many suppliers of lactose-free sour cream. Cultured sour cream is preferred, since bacteria are used in the process. Vinegars are used in non-cultured sour cream.

**CREAM CHEESE** is a low lactose cheese. There are now many suppliers of lactose-free cream cheese.

**Excluded:** Milk, other cheeses, margarine, or other butter substitutes. Avoid rice or soybean substitutes.

### A Word on Kefir and Kombucha

Kefir grains and kombucha scobys are fermented products like yogurt, but whereas yogurt utilizes bacterial fermentation, kefir and kombucha both use bacteria and yeast in their fermentation process. Saccharomyces, the yeast in these products, is the same yeast that is used to make bread, wine, and beer. Ethanol and acetaldehyde are produced by saccharomyces during the fermentation process. Know that acetaldehyde is a known carcinogen, so avoidance is best. Even though ethanol and acetaldehyde are only produced in small quantities in each kefir and kombucha drink, these beverages are currently being heavily promoted for their health benefits, leaving many people to drink kefir and kombucha on a regular basis. I have excluded these products on The Kaufmann Diets.

### Dairy Substitutes

The list of dairy-free cheeses and milk substitutes grows monthly. There are many on the market now. As a general rule, unsweetened goat, coconut, almond, and hemp dairy substitutes are acceptable. Be careful, and read labels for words like casein and whey, as milk can sneak into the product. Check for other un-permitted ingredients, as well.

## 6. Vegetables

**Allowed:** Virtually all fresh, unblemished vegetables. Greens are heavily encouraged. Juicing fresh, organic (preferably) vegetables and spices (ginger/turmeric root) is acceptable.

**Excluded:** Potatoes and sweet potatoes, legumes (including beans, peas, and green beans). Mushrooms and corn are not vegetables and are not allowed.

## 7. Beverages

**Allowed:** Filtered water, fresh-squeezed vegetable juices, and unsweetened herbal teas. Unsweetened almond milk, coconut milk, and various other nut milks are fine.

**Excluded:** All alcoholic beverages are off limits. A component of The Kaufmann 1 Diet involves avoiding foods and drinks that are addictive. For this reason (and others) coffee, regular black tea, and sodas are excluded. Making flavored water beverages yourself with proper ingredients seems to be well tolerated, but please enjoy them in moderation.

8. **Grains**

**Allowed:** Pseudo-grains, such as quinoa, amaranth, buckwheat, and millet. These are actually seeds and not grains.

### A Word on Ancient Grains

Ancient grains are grains that purportedly have not been altered due to selectively breeding. They are still grains, and that needs to be considered. For educational purposes, it is not just the breeding process that is factored in when deciding on grains. Rather, the silo process must also be considered, if this was used. The Kaufmann 1 Diet avoids grains for two distinct reasons: Grains are high in carbohydrates that feed fungi, and they can easily become impregnated with fungi and/or mycotoxins.

**Excluded:** Virtually all grains are excluded. These include corn, wheat, oats, barley, rye, spelt and any foods containing these ingredients, including bread, pasta, cakes, crackers, and other processed foods. Keep in mind that sugar is a grain!

9. **Yeast Products and Fungal Foods**

**Allowed:** None. Be careful of foods that are fermented using yeast. Be vigilant in reading labels, because yeast and its by-products are sometimes cleverly inserted into labels.

**Excluded:** Virtually all products containing yeast are excluded from the diet, including alcohol, bread, etc. Any type of fungus, such as mushrooms and truffles, or foods that might contain fungus or fungal byproducts, such as certain aged cheeses, myco-protein, or nutritional yeasts are to be avoided.

10. **Vinegars/Fermented Food Products**

**Allowed:** Unpasteurized apple cider vinegar. Know that all vinegars are acidic. The fermentation of sugars is used to make vinegar. Apple cider vinegar has been found to have anti-fungal properties against several fungal species, making it allowable. Sauerkraut is a lactic acid product. Lactic acid fermentation creates conditions favorable to lactic acid-producing good microorganisms, like lactobacillus.

**Excluded:** Virtually all others, including other vinegars, most salad dressings or sauces, including soy sauce.

### A Word About Soy Sauce

Soybeans are the 2nd largest crop grown in America, following corn. If you must have soy sauce, try to find the 10% of non-GMO (genetically modified organism) soybeans that exist. The other 90% are GMO soybeans, and according to an educational website, nearly all of that 90% involve the use of a product called Roundup (glyphosate) on the beans, which is a known carcinogen. Know that the darker or thicker soy sauces use molasses or caramel coloring, which is added during the fermentation process. Do your own studies before using soy sauce.

## 11. Oils

**Allowed:** Many oils are allowed, including olive oil, macadamia nut oil, coconut oil, grape seed oil, flax seed oil, etc. Cold-pressed, extra virgin, and minimally processed, organic oils seem to be best.

**Excluded:** Most vegetable oils, hydrogenated oils, corn oil, peanut oil, truffle oil, and canola oil.

### A Word About Canola Oil

Genetically speaking, scientists make canola oil by integrating rapeseed genes with the canola plant genes. Canola oil is rapeseed oil, from which the most toxic monounsaturated omega-9 fatty acid (erucic acid) has been removed through specific breeding. Although rapeseed oil is high in erucic acid, food-grade canola oil is engineered and regulated to contain a maximum of 2% erucic acid in the USA. Europe's equivalent of the United States' FDA states this about erucic acid: "Erucic acid–a naturally occurring contaminant present in vegetable oil–is not a safety concern for most consumers, as the average exposure is less than half the safe level. But, it may be a long-term health risk for children up to 10 years of age who consume high amounts of foods containing this substance."

There are so many great oils we have to choose from. Choose these over others until more is known about their effects on human health.

## 12. Nuts & Seeds

**Allowed:** Nuts and seeds can be problematic for those who suffer from fungal disorders. Broken seeds and/or nut shells expose seeds and nuts to the elements, and one of the elements is fungus. Most nuts and seeds are allowed on the diet, including walnuts, pecans, almonds, cashews, pumpkin seeds, etc. Try to purchase nuts with their shells intact. Of course, this is impossible when purchasing packaged pre-chopped nuts. Be vigilant when buying and eating nuts. You will know when you chew a bad one; spit it out and rinse. Be careful of sunflower seeds, as they can be contaminated with fungus. Freshly ground nut butters are fine, but it is always best to see the nuts being used to make the nut butter. Again, many of us know when we taste a food product if it is contaminated or tastes differently.

**Excluded:** Peanuts (including anything made with peanuts or peanut butter). Science has now published that pistachio nuts and sunflower seeds are sometimes contaminated with fungal mycotoxins, so it is best to avoid those, also.

## The Kaufmann 2 Diet

### 1. Sugar/Sweeteners

**Allowed:** You may experiment with minimal amounts of pure maple syrup and real Manuka honey in moderation, as a trial. Manuka honey has antibacterial and anti-fungal properties, yet some people will be unable to tolerate any honey, or they attempt to challenge it too early in their recovery. When challenging Manuka honey, watch for changes in how you feel afterwards, and base moderate continuation on that.

**Excluded:** All others that were excluded on Kaufmann 1

### 2. Fruit

**Allowed:** Begin adding back fruits on occasion. For example, try red apples on occasion as you begin to add more foods into your diet. Again, watch for symptoms, and know that while a red apple once in a while may be a wonderful treat, eating another the next day might cause some symptoms to return. Do not "load" too quickly.

**Excluded:** The higher sugar content fruits are dates, watermelon, pineapple, and banana, so be cautious of these. Bulk dried fruits are also discouraged, as they run a higher risk for fungal contamination.

### 3. Meat

***Same as Kaufmann 1***

### 4. Eggs

***Same as Kaufmann 1***

### 5. Dairy

**Allowed:** Lower lactose cheeses are OK to experiment with now.

**Excluded:** Milk, other cheeses, margarine, or other butter substitutes. Avoid rice or soybean substitutes.

#### A Word About Cheese

Cheeses that are very low in milk sugar (lactose) are cheddar, Parmesan (very high protein), and Swiss cheeses. As a general rule, aged cheese is low-lactose cheese. Older cheese becomes hard, because it loses its moisture content. With that comes lower milk sugar; therefore, hard cheeses have much less lactose in them. Goat cheeses and milks are generally acceptable, but please be vigilant, as well-meaning nutritional marketers can give hints of cow's milk in their labels.

6. **Vegetables**

   **Allowed:** You are now allowed to include (experiment) with sweet potatoes or yams, and legumes, including beans, peas, etc., in moderation. (Peanuts are still excluded.)

   **Excluded:** Regular potatoes. Although a great source of fiber, potatoes are considered starchy carbohydrates and are 90% sugar and starch (or more). Corn is not a vegetable; it is a grain. Mushrooms are not vegetables; they are fungi. Continue excluding both mushrooms and corn.

7. **Beverages**

   **Allowed:** Since coffee is a bean, you may minimally experiment with coffee now. Be careful, as fungal mycotoxins are sometimes found in coffee beans if their shells crack. Do not go overboard with coffee. If sweetening is desired, use stevia or xylitol.

   **Excluded:** All others excluded on Kaufmann 1

8. **Grains**

   **Allowed:** Experimentation with oats and brown rice is allowed in moderation, because these tend to be less affected by fungus. Again, do not overload on these grains, and revert to Kaufmann 1 should symptoms begin to return.

   **Excluded:** All others excluded on Kaufmann 1

9. **Yeast Products and Fungal Foods**

   ***Allowed and Excluded: Same as Kaufmann 1***

10. **Vinegars/Fermented Food Products**

    ***Allowed and Excluded: Same as Kaufmann 1***

11. **Oils**

    ***Allowed and Excluded: Same as Kaufmann 1***

12. **Nuts & Seeds**

    ***Allowed and Excluded: Same as Kaufmann 1***

# Dietary Additions, 2018

## Hemp Milk, *Kaufmann 1*

As you have learned, cow's milk has several disadvantages over other milks. Dairy is mucous-producing and so often an addictive food in the American diet. Because we consume so many dairy products, it is also one of the most allergic foods, as well. One great alternative is hemp milk. Rich in nutrition, hemp contains all 10 amino acids in addition to minerals like iron, magnesium and potassium and vitamins like the B vitamins. Hemp has another nutritional advantage over cow's milk; it is an excellent source of omega 3 and 6 fatty acids. Because of its nutritional value, many people consider hemp a superfood!

## Maple Syrup, *Kaufmann 2*

Maple syrup is all produced using the same process. The sugar content is also identical at 66.9%. Maple syrup is actually graded by its color, which becomes darker as the weather warms up. It is this darker colored maple syrup that has the strongest flavor.

## Kudzu, *Kaufmann 2*

Roots contain starch and show antioxidant activity. A group of plants from the legume family, kudzu has become a popular source of plant-based remedies. While some remedies are substantiated in the literature, others are not. When cooking, kudzu is an alternative to cornstarch, and it serves to thicken sauces. It is best to buy North American sources, as most imported sources are highly sprayed with herbicides.

## Your Spore Score

Unbeknownst to fungi, they are not here to injure man. Of course, they do, but that is not their primary purpose. Yes, they have adapted to leaning on us for a nice, warm environment and constant food supply, but until they find us, their primary job is to decompose environmental waste. Given the waste in our country alone, fungi must constantly reproduce new workers. They do this by reproducing themselves in a process called sporulation. Fungi make spores to continue their life cycle. The naked eye cannot see fungal spores, but we know that they exist, because they perform their work with great fervor.

Not only are fungi experts at reproducing themselves, but they figured out the idea of taxis long before we did. Once fungal reproduction takes place within the spore, transportation is essential. Fungal "taxi rides" take place in many ways. Birds and bugs can transport their fungal spores for them, but for very long distance travel, spores must rely on their best friend, the wind. With new fallen trees to break down and garbage to decompose, they travel great distances to do their work.

Every physician knows that fungi are responsible for human decomposition after we die, but few know that they are also largely responsible for decomposing our bodies *before we die*. Why is that? In 1999, The World Health Organization (WHO) issued a bulletin that enables all of us who worked in the field of fungal disorders to better understand why we were witnessing such resistance to fungal diagnoses within the medical community. It spoke of *mycotoxicoses*, which are illnesses caused by fungal poisons called mycotoxins. The article stated, *"Mycotoxicoses often remain unrecognized by medical professionals, except when large numbers of people are involved."* (1)

No wonder! Medical offices see one unique patient at a time. If they saw 60 simultaneous patients who were severely bleeding and who all ate peanuts from the same bag, eventually they would figure fungus out.

The fact remains that people are getting better on The Kaufmann Diet and Lifestyle, yet because doctors learned very little about fungus during their medical training, the results I have achieved seem a bit sensational. I recall reading a quote from Kevin Feige around the time I began working in medical clinics and seeing hundreds of sick patients improve on my diet and anti-fungal medications: *"Rejection,"* said Feige, *"is common. Learning that early and often will help you build up the tolerance and resistance to keep going and keep trying."* This saying has continued to inspire me to fight the good fight during the past decades.

A sad commentary on the problem of accurately diagnosing fungal symptoms and diseases was penned in an abstract published in 2004 in a medical journal called *Medical Mycology*. It read, *"...the number of immunocompromised patients and subsequent invasive fungal infections continues to rise. However, the education of future medical mycologists to engage this growing problem is diminishing. While there are an increasing number of publications and grants awarded in mycology, the time and detail devoted to teaching medical mycology in United States medical schools are inadequate."* (2)

Couple this with the difficulty in testing for fungus, and it becomes painfully obvious why we have a fungal health crisis in America. Testing a child's throat for bacteria now takes a few minutes, but testing a child's throat for fungus can take a week. Of course, since physicians learn that infections are primarily bacterial, a demand for an immediate fungal diagnostic test had never been deemed important. Although this is changing, in 2018, much remains the same.

**How Do You Know If Your Health Problems Are Linked To Fungus?**

We have discussed the problem of receiving an accurate fungal diagnosis, although there is a growing number of integrative physicians that are becoming very good at it, and I congratulate them. In all of my teaching seminars during the past 45 years, the inevitable question always arises as to how we lay people might differentiate between fungal symptoms and those caused by bacteria or viruses. When it comes to fungus, *clues are often more accurate than facts*. Read that sentence again. The scientific literature is replete with articles that refer to the diagnostic problems that doctors have when trying to identify fungus as the cause of a variety of health problem. So your hunch that fungus might be the cause of your sinus problem can get you started on reversing the problem before a diagnosis is reached.

Here is some information from an infographic that I recently prepared for educational purposes. I tried to point out that while fungi are truly the root cause of much human suffering, they often masquerade as catastrophic disorders:

> *Recent scientific publications state that fungal infections mimic colorectal cancer, skeletal tuberculosis, Ewing's sarcoma, bone cancer, lupus, gram-negative bacterial infection, lung cancer, thyroid mass, Alzheimer's disease, tendonitis, Crohn's disease, lacrimal sac abscess, clostridium difficile infection, osteomyelitis, chronic sinusitis.*

Yes, each of these illnesses—and more—can be masquerading as a life threatening disease, but are sometimes nothing more than a treatable fungal infection.

Clostridium difficile can be misdiagnosed? Is that not the "bacteria" that causes diarrhea? Indeed it is, but fungi can also induce diarrhea. Perhaps one day someone will redefine gram negative "bacteria" as fungi or mycotoxins. Medical education expounds on bacteriology rather than mycology for a reason, as there are hundreds of antibiotics on the market today and only a handful of anti-fungal medications. This lack of drug equality tends to indoctrinate young medical students that disease-causing bacteria are a huge problem, while disease-causing fungi are not. Given this, it is important that you understand how your lifestyle might have set you up for a fungal illness, be it a local skin disorder, or a deeper fungal condition that is now masquerading as a serious disease. You could have a chronic mycotoxicosis that is masquerading, and has been erroneously diagnosed, as a life threatening illness. A simple questionnaire might assist some of you in better knowing if your symptoms or diseases are linked to fungus.

---

*References:*

(1) Peraica, M, et al. "Toxic Effects of Mycotoxins in Humans." *Bulletin of the World Health Organization*, vol. 77, no. 9, 1977, pp. 754–756.

(2) Steinbach, William J., et al. "Status of Medical Mycology Education." *Medical Mycology*, vol. 41, no. 6, 2003, pp. 457–467., doi:10.1080/13693780310001631322.

# Your Spore Score

By no means is this questionnaire diagnostic. Based upon research concerning known fungal risk factors, the questionnaire is used to assess the degree to which you may have been exposed to fungi, and the odds that fungi or their mycotoxins lie behind a given problem. Consider it a "ball-parker" to assist you and your doctor in more accurately understanding the role that fungus might have in your health condition. This questionnaire and a careful medical history that covers questions like these can be of tremendous value to the diagnostician.

1. At any time in your life, have you taken repeated or prolonged rounds of antibiotics?

   ______________________________________________

2. Are you allergic to any medications? Please specify.

   ______________________________________________

3. At any time in your life, have you taken repeated or prolonged courses of steroids or cortisone-based pills?

   ______________________________________________

4. Do you have fingernail/toenail or scalp fungus?

   ______________________________________________

5. Have you ever had ringworm or other skin problems?

   ______________________________________________

6. Had you spent time in a construction site when your illness began?

   ______________________________________________

7. Have you ever slept or spent time in a basement?

   ______________________________________________

8. Do you have breathing problems like COPD or chronic sinusitis?

______________________________________________

9. Does your job place you underneath buildings or underground?

______________________________________________

10. Do you suffer from dandruff?

______________________________________________

11. Have you been diagnosed with attention deficit disorder (ADD) or hyperactivity?

______________________________________________

12. Do your bones, muscles or joints bother you?

______________________________________________

13. Do you have a chronic cough?

______________________________________________

14. Do you suffer from fatigue? Circle your energy level (10 is lowest).
    **1 2 3 4 5 6 7 8 9 10**

15. Do you often feel irritable?

______________________________________________

16. Do you often feel dazed or "spaced out?"

______________________________________________

17. Do you suffer from memory loss?

______________________________________________

18. Have you ever had chronic sinusitis?

______________________________________________

19. Do your ears chronically itch?

______________________________________________

20. Do you eat breakfast cereals, bread, pasta, or pastries daily?

_______________

21. Do you crave sugar?

_______________

22. How many glasses of alcohol do you drink weekly, on average?

_______________

23. Have you ever been treated for parasites or worms?

_______________

24. Have you been diagnosed with diabetes?

_______________

25. Have you been diagnosed with cancer?

_______________

26. Have you been diagnosed with migraine or hormonal headaches?

_______________

27. Do you have seasonal or “all-the-time” allergies?

_______________

28. Do you have high cholesterol/triglycerides?

_______________

29. Are you bothered by recurring problems with your digestive tract such as bloating, belching, gas, constipation, diarrhea, abdominal pain, indigestion, or reflux?

_______________

30. Have you ever been diagnosed with an autoimmune disease? Specify the disease, including when you were diagnosed.

_______________

31. Do you feel worse on overcast or rainy days?

___

32. Does your skin itch after a bath or shower?

___

33. Have you ever been diagnosed with depression?

___

34. Has a home you have lived in ever experienced a mold problem, or leaked? When?

___

35. Do fabric store odors, smoke, or chemical smells bother you?

___

36. Do you have food allergies?

___

37. Have you been diagnosed with a neurological illness?

___

## For Women Only

1. Has a mammogram identified "calcification" or ductal carcinoma in-situ?

___

2. Have you ever taken birth control pills? Did they cause complications?

___

3. Have you experienced uterine, vaginal, or urinary tract problems such as endometriosis, polycystic ovarian syndrome, UTIs, or fibroids?

___

## For Men Only

1. Do you have chronic testicular pain?

   ______________________________

2. Do you have prostate problems or an elevated PSA?

   ______________________________

3. Do you experience male hormonal disturbances like loss of libido, infertility, or impotence?

   ______________________________

## How To Interpret This Questionnaire

Once again, know that no matter what your score on this questionnaire, you did not pass or fail, because the Spore Score is scoreless! The results mean so much more than a score would. They finally give you subjective data that you have never had before that can definitely help with an accurate diagnosis. Based on this simple questionnaire you now have relevant, fungal-based information to assist you in defining the probability that fungus or fungal mycotoxins might or might not be contributing to your health conditions.

Obviously, if you have scored a "0" on this questionnaire, it is unlikely (but not impossible) that your health conditions could be linked to fungus. Conversely, a score of 40 does not automatically implicate fungus as the cause of your health problems, although it is very likely that it is. Your Spore Score, therefore, must be taken in context with other factors, like your age, weight, exercise program, and lifestyle in order to better interpret it. The most important missing data on the questionnaire has to do with what is written on the pages of your personal doctor's office patient chart. Couple this score with your medical record information, and you have got some very valuable data that will help your doctor accurately diagnose your condition. For your doctor, this test is a "ball-parker," but for you, I know it was an "eye-opener!"

# Who Is Doug Kaufmann?

1968 was a frightening time for an American 18-year-old boy. The Vietnam War was being ramped up, and we could all watch the carnage of helicopters and body bags on the 6 o'clock news each night. My friends were getting draft notices, and within months, being sent to Vietnam. In lieu of accepting that plight, I quickly enlisted in the U.S. Navy, where I became convinced that the very worst thing that could happen to me was to be stationed on a U.S. Navy ship somewhere near Vietnam. I could do that! Anchors away!

I served in the U.S. Navy from 1968-1972 as a hospital corpsman. I had no idea what a hospital corpsman even was, but I knew that every Navy ship had at least one of them on it, so I still felt safe! Somewhere in all of this, I learned that hospital corpsmen served in combat duty with The U.S. Marine Corps. In that capacity, I was trained in emergency medicine and served in Vietnam with the 7th Marines, both in the field, and at the First Medical Battalion Hospital in Danang. I left for Vietnam about 2 years into my four-year obligation to the Navy.

I returned home to Los Angeles from Vietnam in 1971 at the age of 21. That age is relevant to my story and my discovery, as you will learn.

If you have ever experienced a monsoon weather pattern like those seen in Vietnam, you know how miserable they can be. Now, imagine a rain-filled monsoon weather front that lasts an entire week or two. Strong wind and drenching rain are the standard. Imagine a few more things: living outside during that week with no daylight 50% of the time, no walls, no heat, no change of clothes or shoes, no bathroom, and knowing that you might be surrounded by people who want to kill you. Ok, now you've got it.

Those stresses have much to do with what we Americans have called post traumatic stress disorder, or PTSD. PTSD messes with your mind, but so does neurotoxic fungus. This is where my age becomes relevant to this story and to my discovery. Recall that we stayed wet for weeks at a time without changing our clothes. This gave us the strangest rashes you had ever seen. Jungle rot is a type of fungus that was common in Vietnam, and I had my share of it. Jungle rot doesn't stay in Vietnam. You bring it home with you. Certain germs can enter our bodies transdermally, and I am 100% convinced that this was the way that fungus gained access to the inside of me so long ago.

Loud noises setting us off is a given for every combat action veteran and very understandable. But within several months of my return from Vietnam, my arms started bleeding. I began having horrible gut problems, and I began experiencing paranoia problems, especially when getting into an elevator with other people. There were other problems, too. I simply began climbing the 9 floors of stairs in the medical school I worked in upon returning home, rather than ride up the elevator. But it was more complicated than these symptoms, and that would take me some years to piece together.

Simultaneous to my having these strange symptoms was the fact that I was now 21 years old. California sets the minimum age to buy or consume alcohol at 21 years. I now realize that this age of consent formed the perfect storm inside my body. You see, our immune systems can fend off fungal infections, unless we disallow it to. Fungi must have beer—lots of beer and other carbohydrates—to thrive inside our bodies. I didn't know that in 1971. But by simply combining my oozing fungal problems with their favorite food (carbohydrates) I had ensured my continue suffering. Of course, what respectable 21-year-old man drinks beer without Mexican food? Soon, corn tortillas and chips and more beer, cookies, tacos, beer, soda, sugar, beer (you get my point) ignited my health problems, and the cycle of chronic illness began. I was owned by fungus, and I believe many of you reading this book are also owned by fungus.

I figured that if diet could feed my illness, could a different diet starve it? Indeed it can! Even today, few know that fungi are human parasites, and as such, they must eat or they will die. Without carbohydrates, like those hops, malt, and barley in beer, they slowly become defeated. Armed with this information in the 1970s, I began building a diet that could, I hoped, literally starve fungi.

This discovery will one day change physicians' denial that diet plays a role in their patients' suffering. The good news is that many are now placing their patients on The Kaufmann 1 Diet, and the results speak for themselves.

As you partake of this diet, know three things. First, if you have a medical condition and are on medication, please get your doctor's approval to follow this diet. He/she knows your medical history, and I do not. Second, deeper or very long-term fungal growth may require the use of anti-fungal medication along with this diet. If, within a few weeks you are not feeling improvement on the diet alone, you might inquire about taking a systemic anti-fungal medication like Diflucan or Sporanox from your doctor. The doctors I worked with always prescribed the gut anti-fungal drug, Nystatin, along with the Diflucan or Sporanox. Third and finally, give it the old "college try," but know that many people experience a "die off" reaction, which is also called a Herxheimer reaction. This is a "healing crisis" and it may last for a few days before you wake up feeling much better. Generally, within a week, some feel better, within 2 weeks more feel better, and within 4 weeks the majority feel much better. A month on the diet cures nothing, but at least your years of misery finally has a name! Starving fungus has you feeling so much better. This is your wake up call for more of the same until you have recovered.

Let me emphasize this final statement, because it is the platform of this entire diet and manuscript: For you or me not to understand this food-fungus cycle of illness is understandable. I believe it is incomprehensible, however, for those trained in medicine to not know the obvious dietary link to fungal disorders. The good news is that more and more are now witnessing it, because patients like you are educating them. Like I once was, you may be suffering from a systemic fungal disorder, driven by your diet and not even know it. For this reason, the book you hold in your hands could be life-changing and even lifesaving. Once you experience the power of this diet, it is incumbent upon you to share it with loved ones. Thank you in advance!

# Contributors

## Joy Miller

Joy Miller is the wife of John Miller, the producer of *Know The Cause*, the television show. Joy learned how to cook from her father at an early age. After learning about the fungus link to disease, Joy has cultivated her own way of cooking that fits within The Kaufmann Diets. Joy also assists people with Alzheimers and dementia.

---

## Abby Miller

Abby is the daughter of John Miller, the producer of *Know The Cause*. She is a realtor in the Dallas/Fort Worth region, a certified Level 1 Crossfit trainer, dog owner, and an avid experimenter with food. Abby learned to cook while growing up in the kitchen with her mom and grandparents and implemented The Kaufmann Diet into her life when her father started working for *Know The Cause*.

---

## Lindsey Crouch

Guiltless Goodies

www.guiltlessgoodies.com

Lindsey Crouch is mom of 3, wife, entrepreneur, recipe developer, and co-founder of the world's first seed-only flour and foods company, 7 Seed Foods. She was inspired to create nutrient-dense foods after losing her mom to cancer at a young age and to support her husband in his health, wellness, and fitness journey. Lindsey and husband Daniel own a bakery and manufacturing plant in Austin, Tx where they make all of their 7 Seed products. They love working together to make healthy living more accessible to everyone everywhere.

---

## Melissa Henig

www.rawpaleo.com

Melissa Henig is a health and lifestyle coach, researcher, mother, and into everything natural. She is the author of the book, *Raw Paleo*. Her coaching program gets women and men to feel strong and vibrant.

---

## Kristin Hoedebeck

Kristin Hoedebeck is a wife, mother of two, and has worked with *Know The Cause* for 18 years. She loves to cook for her family and enjoys having her kids help in the kitchen.

---

## Damon Black

Damon Black is a production manager at *Know The Cause*. He has been in the film and TV industry for several years with most of his background in the computer video industry. Cooking started as a hobby to unwind which grew into experimentation and adapting recipes to be Kaufmann Diet friendly.

---

# NOTES

# NOTES

# NOTES

# NOTES

# NOTES

# NOTES

# NOTES

# NOTES

# NOTES

# NOTES